Critical Thinking
for A2

More related titles

Critical Thinking for AS Level
Roy van den Brink-Budgen

Critical Thinking for Students
Learn the skills of critical assessment and effective argument

'A really useful introduction to developing and improving a core skill.'
– Association of Commonwealth Universities Bulletin

How to Pass Exams Every Time
Proven techniques for any exam that will boost your confidence and guarantee success

'If you want a book that is excellently written and will show you how to study and approach exams, buy this!' – Amazon reviewer

Writing an Essay
Simple techniques to transform your coursework and examinations

'There is a lot of good sense in this book.' – Times Educational Supplement

howtobooks
Send for a free copy of the latest catalogue to:
How To Books
3 Newtec Place, Magdalen Road,
Oxford OX4 1RE, United Kingdom
email: info@howtobooks.co.uk
http://www.howtobooks.co.uk

Critical Thinking
for A2

R o y   v a n   d e n   B r i n k - B u d g e n

howtobooks

DEDICATION

To the Critical Thinkers of the future:
Hannie, Daisy, Noah, Darcey, Martha, Eleanor, Ruby, Thomas, and Ptolemy

Published by How To Books Ltd,
3 Newtec Place, Magdalen Road,
Oxford, OX4 1RE, United Kingdom
Tel: (01865) 793806 Fax: (01865) 248780
email: info@howtobooks.co.uk
http://www.howtobooks.co.uk

First edition 2006

British Library Cataloguing in Publication Data
A catalogue record for this book is available from
the British Library.

Produced for How To Books by Deer Park Productions, Tavistock
Typeset by *specialist* publishing services ltd, Montgomery/Milton Keynes
Cover design by Baseline Arts Ltd, Oxford
Printed and bound by Bell & Bain Ltd, Glasgow

CONTENTS

PREFACE

Those of you who have read my 'Critical Thinking for AS Level' will know something of what to expect with this book. You will know that we don't go in for little boxes pushing handy (blindingly obvious) hints in your direction. You will know that you're treated as someone with sufficient intelligence to be able to handle this subject. Furthermore, unlike others who attempt to help you to look at the subject of Critical Thinking at this level, I am sure that you enjoy demands being made of you.

This book gives you all you need for success in the A2 course. It covers all the information and explanations that are necessary. It also gives you lots of examples and exercises so that you can practise and further develop your skills. But I hope that it also serves another purpose. That is, to show you that the subject is one of enormous importance. There is much value in being able to think with care, to think with regard to other possibilities and other explanations. The subject therefore earns its keep many times over.

I continue to work with many hundreds of students all around the country, and with many of the teachers who teach them. As a result, I hope that I very much understand the needs of both groups. I write my books in order to meet these needs. One teacher wrote to me earlier this year to say that he was delighted with my book for the AS course because 'It makes such a change to have a book that doesn't patronise students and teachers'. I was very pleased to get this comment because it gave me some evidence (albeit limited!) that I'd got it right.

So be prepared to not be patronised. Be prepared to be taken as a bright, skilled thinker who has decided to raise their game. Be prepared to see the world differently once you've finished. And be prepared for success.

Then you too will suffer exasperation when faced with daily absurdities like being asked recently by *The Times* if I'd 'like to holiday like the Queen?' (yes please) or the man who explained to me whilst I was walking my dog that 'smacking doesn't do anybody any harm. My dad was smacked as a child and he lived until he was 87'.

As the rather less absurd thinker, Hannibal Lecter, said, 'See you around.'

PART I / UNIT 3
RESOLUTION OF DILEMMAS

INTRODUCTION: WHAT IS THIS UNIT CONCERNED WITH?

Critical Thinking is very much concerned with analysing and evaluating arguments that we find in the real world. Though we might sometimes say things like 'If x is the case, then y is the case …', we do this only to clarify what's going on in an argument. The following example should show this.

> *Though we're not sure whether global warming will develop over the next fifty years, we can work out what will happen if it does. Suppose that temperatures rise even by only a couple of degrees, then ice must melt. Given a situation in which ice is melting, then sea levels must rise. So, whatever else happens (for example, whether or not Northern Europe will be warmer or colder as a result of global warming), global warming must lead to flooding along many coastlines. So it is foolish to buy a property near a coastline.*

This argument is, as you can see, dealing with what would happen if global warming takes place. It's an example of hypothetical reasoning, such that if x happens, then y happens, and if y happens, then z happens. Seeing it like that can make it easier to see why the conclusion is overdrawn. The conclusion is not a hypothetical one (if there were to be such flooding, it would be foolish to buy a property near a coastline), whereas the rest of the argument is.

This example showed us that, though we might occasionally use symbols to analyse and evaluate arguments, the content of the arguments is concerned with the real world. The unit entitled 'Resolution of Dilemmas' does the same thing. It is concerned with making decisions about real problems.

Though politicians are often criticised for the decisions they make, it has to be accepted that, at some point, politicians do have to make decisions about such problems as crime, university funding, health care, GM foods, and so on. They are often faced with having to make decisions that will upset one group or another. For example, the Government announced in December 2005 that they are proposing to

1

allow the killing of a large number of badgers in various parts of the country in 2006. They have done this in large part because farming groups are sure that badgers spread bovine tuberculosis to cattle. However, the evidence is strongly disputed by animal welfare groups. So, the Government is faced with a problem. Should it do what the farmers want or what the animal welfare groups (and the majority of the public) want? How does it decide between the two positions? What range of options is available to the Government? Allow the killing of badgers only in areas affected by bovine TB? Allow only an experiment lasting a few months?

This example of the proposed killing of badgers illustrates very well how decision-making can involve a number of stages. We could see the problem to be addressed in the following way.

- What range of policies is available?

- What sort of evidence is relevant?

- What does the evidence tell us?

- How do we decide between different positions?

- What decision can best be defended?

Within some of the questions, there are issues that need to be addressed. For example, though we have referred to the 'killing' of badgers, the official word is 'culling'. Is the difference in wording significant? Does 'culling' not mean 'killing'? The Concise Oxford Dictionary gives 'to cull' as meaning 'select from flock, etc. and kill (surplus animals, etc.)'. So culling does mean killing, but killing with a particular purpose. Here we have an example where the meaning of a term is significant. We shall be examining the issue of problems of meaning in Chapter One on 'definitions'.

You can see that the questions are designed to lead us towards making the best decision. Looking at what options are available is a good example of Critical Thinking in action. You will probably be familiar with the term 'restricting the options' or 'false dilemma' (if necessary, remind yourself by looking at pages 103-104 of *Critical Thinking for AS Level*). Instead of saying that we can either kill badgers or do nothing, we could consider looking to see if bovine TB is caused by other factors (such as other wild animals, or by cattle infecting each other). We could also look at the possibility of vaccinating cattle against bovine TB.

Looking at evidence takes us to the centre of Critical Thinking. We know that we need to ask questions about the evidence used in any argument. Is it relevant? Does it do what the author intends it to? (In other words, what significance does the evidence have?) What other evidence would be relevant?

When we are faced with different options for action, having considered the evidence available, we often use a framework for making the decision. For example, when unmanned level crossings were introduced, part of what was considered was how many people were likely to be injured or killed by introducing them. Clearly, unmanned level crossings saved money by getting rid of the need to pay someone to open and close the gates, but could this saving be balanced against the increased risk to the public? A figure was calculated for numbers injured and killed. Then a figure was given for the value of a human life (in terms of its economic value: income lost, family support costs, etc.). The resulting calculation showed that unmanned level crossings could be justified in economic terms. So they were introduced.

In this example, an economic framework was used to make the decision. If a moral framework had been used, a different decision might or might not have been made. If we can never justify risking serious injury or death to people, then unmanned level crossings cannot be justified. On the other hand, the savings to public expenditure could be justified morally by having to take less money from people through their taxes.

In the end, then, your task in the 'Resolution of Dilemmas' unit is to take yourself to a decision. Faced with a choice between policies or positions, which one can be better justified? It is then very much Critical Thinking in action. This is especially the case when we consider the sort of issues that you might deal with.

- Should we use animals in medical experiments?

- What should be done about poverty in the developing world?

- Should we encourage the development of GM food as a way of feeding the world?

- Should we force people to save for their retirement?

- Should we refuse to treat on the NHS those who smoke?

- Should young people who don't go to university be expected to pay with their taxes for those who do?

All of these issues will benefit from going though the process that we considered on page 2 (range of policies, evidence, etc.). As you might be able to see, a range of responses to the problems is possible. Hopefully, working out what to do with this range will turn out to be an exciting and worthwhile task. Critical Thinking should be both exciting and worthwhile. Let's make a start on doing this task. We'll look at the question of definitions first.

1
DEFINITIONS

In my book for the AS course, we looked briefly at the subject of definitions. There we established that the way an author uses definitions can play a very important part in their argument. We saw how the terms 'safe', 'fit', and 'environment' were all used in ways that were not necessarily straightforward. (You might need to remind yourself of how we did this.)

PROBLEMS OF DEFINITION

In picking up the subject of definitions again, we will see that the way an author uses words can create all sorts of problems in an argument. We'll start with a very simple example.

We're all winners with the National Lottery.

This comforting message was seen on a car sticker. It is not difficult to see that the word 'winners' is problematic. If I were to say to my family that I was a winner with the National Lottery, they are likely to imagine a life of Riley opening up before them. If I then went on to explain that our local park is going to receive some Lottery funding (which it is), then their excitement at winning will be considerably reduced. A renovated old wooden shelter is a poor substitute for a promised life of Riley. So the car sticker might at one level be giving a powerful message, but the power lies in the obvious (and deliberate) ambiguity of the word 'winner'.

Of course, some words or terms are entirely straightforward in terms of definition. Take the word 'cauliflower' for example. If I serve you with a plate of carrots covered with cheese sauce, and say 'here's a lovely plate of cauliflower cheese', something very odd is going on. For whatever reason, I am using words wrongly. The difference between a cauliflower and a carrot is clear. There is no obvious problem in agreeing what is the definition of a cauliflower.

DEFINING FREEDOM

But not everything is so simple. Read the following passage. It was written by Benito Mussolini, the Fascist leader of Italy between 1922 and 1944.

> ... *the fascist conception of life stresses the importance of the State and accepts the individual only in so far as his interests coincide with those of the State ... if liberty is to be the attribute of living men and not of abstract dummies ... then fascism stands for liberty, and for the only liberty worth having, the liberty of the State and of the individual within the State.* [1]

Now read the next one. This was written by John Stuart Mill, a very important British philosopher who lived between 1806 and 1873.

> *The only freedom which deserves the name is that of pursuing our own good in our own way, so long as we do not attempt to deprive others of theirs, or impede their efforts to obtain it.* [2]

The John Stuart Mill excerpt comes from an essay he wrote 'On Liberty'. So if we agree that he and Mussolini are both talking about 'liberty' or 'freedom', then what is going on?

Fascism, as Mussolini explains, sees individuals as having significance only if they fit with what the State demands. The State is everything. J S Mill's account obviously sees individuals very differently. The idea of having a right to pursue 'our own good in our own way' is a contradiction of what the fascist believes. With Mussolini, the State defines what is good for us, what we ought to want to do, not us as individuals. So can liberty be both what the fascist sees it as, and what a liberal like J S Mill sees it as? Can it just mean anything that anyone chooses to make it?

Here we have an example then where a word or term is being used in ways that show us that there is a problem.

If we look at our everyday meanings of the word 'free', then we might be able to cut through the problem. Look at the following ways in which the word appears.

Free gift
Free of charge
Free period
Free for all
Free speech

What is a feature of the word 'free' as it is used in these ways? What, for example, is it about a free period that's like free speech? The short answer is that, in each case, we're looking for a lack of restriction of some sort.

A free gift is an odd term. When you give a gift, you give it without expecting the recipient to pay for it. 'Here's a gift for your birthday, so that's £15 you owe me' is a contradiction. So, the idea of a 'gift' already contains within it the idea of no charge. What could a gift be like that had a restriction or encumbrance? When an elderly relative gives you £5 for your birthday with the comment 'Don't spend it on rubbish', then the gift in one sense is less free. It comes with a restriction. What about promises that you get through the post or see in shops 'Spend £25 and get a free gift'?

'Free of charge' points to what we're looking for. A charge in this case is a cost or price. When this book is published I get ten copies free of charge. They arrive through the post, without my having to pay anything. There is no restriction on my receiving them. What about the BOGOFs (Buy One, Get One Free) so common in supermarkets? Is the one free of charge, free in the same sense as my parcel of books? Not really, in that the free bottle of shampoo is free only if I've bought the first. So it's free of charge only when I've done something, when I've accepted the encumbrance of a price on the first bottle of shampoo. (You might want to say that my parcel of books is not free in the same sense that I've had to accept the encumbrance of writing it in the first place. But this does seem rather different.)

'Free period' is, as you will obviously know, a term used to describe time in a timetable when you have no scheduled lessons. A scheduled lesson is therefore encumbered in the sense that you have to be somewhere, doing something, at a particular time. A 'free period' is a slot of time without such encumbrances. This is not to say that there are no encumbrances (such as restrictions on what you can be doing during this time), but there are none of the encumbrances that come from a timetabled lesson. In other words, 'free' here refers to an absence of relevant encumbrances.

'Free speech' is an interesting term. What might we be looking at here? Following our previous discussion, we are presumably looking for speech that has (or should have) no encumbrances. Thus, if you have 'free speech', does this mean that you can say what you like? Can you shout 'Fire!' in a packed cinema when there is no fire? Can you sing 'Chelsea are the greatest football team' amongst the Manchester United fans at Old Trafford? In each case, you obviously can, but in each case it would probably be better if you didn't. The encumbrance that would follow the second example is that you might be actively encouraged to be quiet. The encumbrance in the first is that you might be prosecuted for causing the panic (and possible injury) that follows your action.

So, when we're talking about 'free speech', are we talking about speech without any encumbrance? This example illustrates our problem. At one level we know what we mean. At another level, we're not sure. This is what makes the term a problematic one to define.

Do the same exercise as above with any other examples you can think of in the use of the word 'free' (and versions such as 'freedom' and 'freely').

Why, then, is the term 'free' problematic for definition?

- It is used in ways that people would not all agree on.

- Going on from this, it can be used in contradictory ways.

- It can be used vaguely.

- It can be used by the same people to mean one thing and then another. For example, when people say that we should have 'free speech', are they using the term in the same way as when they refer to something being 'free of charge'?

- It can be used in ways that appear to not make sense. For example, are you free to buy a new Rolls Royce? In one sense, of course you are. There are no restrictions on your buying one, just as there are no restrictions on your buying a CD. Are you free to buy alcohol? No, if you are under 18. If you think again about the Rolls Royce example, is the point about encumbrances helpful here? Yes, you are free to go to a Rolls Royce dealer today to order the best in the range, but you probably lack the opportunity to do this because of your lack of sufficient funds.

This examination of the term 'free(dom)' should show us how to approach a question about why a particular word/term/phrase is problematic.

PRACTISING WITH DEFINITIONS

It would be useful to practise this skill in looking at why terms are problematic to define. To do this, you need to think of those where the definition isn't straightforward. The following are examples.

- Justice (including 'social justice')

- Peace

- Poverty

- Education

- Happiness

- Crime

- Security

FINDING THE PROBLEMATIC TERM

Sometimes, we use terms as if they are unambiguous when, in fact, they are far from being clear. For example, if we use the term 'human rights', what ambiguity might there be? Interestingly, there is little or no ambiguity about the term 'rights'. We could define it in terms of 'entitlement'. Thus if someone or something (a group of people, for example) has a right to x, then we are saying that they are entitled to x. There might be problems about implementation (who has a duty to provide this entitlement?), but that doesn't make the term 'right' a problematic one to define. In addition, what the right is to (liberty, adequate food, education, health care, and so on) might be disputed, but that is a different issue. The term 'right' is not in itself problematic for definition as a result.

However, the term 'human' raises problems. Why is it problematic?

It is problematic at a number of levels. Consider the following questions.

- When does the quality of 'human' start? At conception? At so many weeks after conception? When the foetus could survive independently of the mother?

- How can we define what it is to be 'human'? Is it to do with physical characteristics, intellectual characteristics, or both, or other criteria?

- Is 'human' simply an entry on a continuum, close to the higher apes?

Though this is not the place to provide an answer to these questions, it is worthwhile considering how they make the term 'human' problematic. These problems can be focused into the question 'What does the term "human" mean?'

Here's one possible answer.

The term 'human' means $H_{1570}N_{310}O_{6500}C_{2250}Ca_{63}P_{48}K_{15}S_{15}Na_{10}C_{16}Mg_3Fe_1$. This is the chemical formula for the human body.[3] So just as the term 'water' can be accurately defined as H_2O, can we define 'human' in terms of the chemical composition of humans?

What happens if someone loses arms or legs? If their chemical composition has changed, are they less 'human'? Given that male bodies contain more water than those of females, is this a problem for a definition of 'human'?

This very short consideration of the problem of defining 'human' shows that, though the term 'right' is not problematic, the term 'human right' is problematic because of the difficulties of nailing down what we mean by 'human'.

FINDING PROBLEMS WITHIN THE DEFINITION

Another feature that can make definitions problematic is that, even if the definition itself is acceptable by most people, the significance of the detail of the definition might be less straightforward. For example, if we look for a definition of the word 'punishment' in the Concise Oxford Dictionary, we find 'penalty inflicted on offender'. This is an unsurprising definition and, given that it comes from the Oxford Dictionary, one would expect it to be an accurate one.

The reason why the definition is problematic is that we would not all agree on the significance of the word 'penalty'. This disagreement can be found being played out in various newspapers. Some will complain bitterly that penalties given to many offenders are not punishments at all. For example, I used to teach at a prison called Hollesley Bay. *The News of the World* called this place 'Holiday Bay' after detailing revelations of prisoners having a comfortable life, with access to alcohol and an apparently willing female staff member. So 'Holiday Bay' would not be seen as punishment. Even very long sentence tariffs of thirty or more years that are given to some murderers are not seen as proper penalties by some people (who declare that 'life should mean life'). Interestingly, some prisoners will also take issue with the notion of a 'penalty'. One burglar I spoke to saw his three year sentence as no more than an 'occupational hazard' which was entirely manageable: 'you get a warm room, a bed, three meals a day, and education, all for free!'.

SUMMARY

We have been looking at what makes the definition of some terms problematic. Though this is a different task to trying to define something, the two very often run together. In other words, the fact that we find it difficult to nail something down to a straightforward definition does indicate that a term might be problematic to define. But a question that asks you to explain why a term is problematic to define is not asking you to provide an answer that does no more than give a definition. It is asking you to explain why any definition is problematic.

This can be done in a number of ways.

- The term can be used ambiguously.

- The term can be used in a way that is vague.

- The term can mean very different things to different people.

- The term can be too open-ended such that its meaning is unclear (as in 'free speech').

- The term can be given a definition upon which many people would agree, but the detailed content of the definition can cause disagreements.

ACTIVITY 1

The term 'health' is problematic to define. Explain why this is so. In your answer, you should consider the following questions.
- What should a definition of 'health' contain?
- How does a definition fit with what can realistically be achieved?
- Should it have to fit as above?
- Is health the absence or presence of something (or both)?
- Should a definition of 'health' be applicable to all situations?

Remember that your task is to show why 'health' is problematic to define. This might involve you trying to define it, but that would be only as a means of showing that there are problems with definition. Essentially, you are showing why we might not all agree with a definition because of the nature of the thing being defined.

ACTIVITY 1: COMMENTARY

We can start by considering definitions of 'health' that are already available. The most often-quoted and used is that of the World Health Organisation (WHO) which was given in 1948.

Health is a state of complete physical, mental and social well-being and not merely the absence of disease or infirmity.

Why might this definition be a problem?

- It is a very demanding definition, with its emphasis on 'complete'.

- It includes things in the definition that might be seen as going beyond what we would normally see as 'health' ('social well-being').

- It is difficult to achieve. How often do you feel in a state of 'complete physical, mental and social well-being'?

- Though we might understand what 'physical well-being' means, what does a 'complete' version mean: never a twinge or ache?

- The term 'mental well-being' might cause problems. Does it allow for any stress (such as waiting in a queue, or being annoyed at something)?

- What does 'social well-being' mean?

- It gives a definition that makes it difficult to measure improvements. We might, for example, improve physical well-being but not social well-being.

These issues illustrate what makes 'health' difficult to define. Just in trying to define it, we find ourselves caught up with problems.

Other problems with definition come from what is sometimes given as a negative and a positive definition of health.

- A negative definition stresses the absence of something (disease, ill-health, etc.).

- A positive definition stresses the achievement of something (well-being, good health, etc.)

We can see why the word 'free' is often used to refer to health. For example, it could be defined in the following way.

Health is being free from disease, whether physical or mental.

How does this definition fit with our earlier discussion of the term 'free'?

There is a very important feature of the problem of defining health. This is whether the definition can be (has to be?) an absolute one or whether it can be (has to be?) a relative one. For example, the WHO definition is an absolute one: it sets a standard whatever the situation. But that could be seen as very problematic.

- Would we be able to adapt a definition to fit with all of the following: individuals, groups (say, families), areas and regions, countries?

- Would we able to fit a definition to changes over time? An absolute one (like the WHO) is independent of changes over time. Does this make sense, given that in many ways, health improves over time? Must we have a definition that fits only with what people's perception of health is at any one time?

- Would we be able to fit a definition to variations between societies? For example, is what is considered healthy in one country going to be considered healthy in another?

- Would we be able to fit a definition to different age-groups? For example, is health the same for an 18 year-old as for a 58 year-old as for an 88 year-old?

A different question is whether statistical evidence can inform our concern about how health should be defined. Does such evidence make the definition more or less problematic?

If statistical evidence has value here, what sort would we need to apply to our definition? The most commonly reported types of evidence are:

- Life expectancy

- Death rates

- Infant mortality rates

- Death rates by specific diseases

On this basis we find the following:[4]

- Andorra has the highest life expectancy in the world (83.5 years for a child born today).

- Swaziland has the lowest life expectancy in the world (29.9 years for a child born today).

- United Arab Emirates has the lowest death rate in the world (as measured by number of deaths per 1000 population), with the figure of 1.3.

- Swaziland has the highest death rate in the world, with a figure of 31.2.

- Hungary has the highest death rate from lung cancer in the world.

- Swaziland has the highest death rates from TB and HIV/AIDS in the world.

- The US has the highest rate of spending on health (at 14.6 % of GDP).

- Iraq has the lowest rate of spending on health (at 1.5% of GDP).

Questions about our definition about health that arise from this sort of evidence could include the following.

- Is the death rate from lung cancer a good way of measuring a country's health?

- Is long life expectancy a guarantee of good health?

- Can health be measured in terms of the amount spent on health care?

- Can we take a definition of health and apply it to countries as diverse as Swaziland and Andorra?

- Is Andorra a healthy society?

 This type of question shows why health is problematic to define. Though at one level, we all know what it is, the problems of definition are considerable.

These problems make it difficult for governments to be seen as being able to be credited with improving health. What sort of decisions would governments need to make to achieve greater health in the population? If it's to increase spending, wouldn't we expect to find the US as the healthiest society, given that it spends the most? Unfortunately, it's not as simple as that. Though the US has a better death rate than the UK (and lots of other European countries such as Switzerland, France, and Sweden), it has a slightly worse one than India. It also has a relatively high death rate from lung cancer and a fairly high rate of diabetes in the population (at a rate the same as India).

You might remember that in my book *Critical Thinking for AS Level* (p. 116), we considered an argument that gave a definition of 'safe'. This was that 'something is safe if the risk attached to it of something unwelcome happening is acceptably low.' This illustrated the problem of defining something in absolute terms. The same point is relevant to 'health'. As an absolute (like the WHO definition), it is unreachable for most situations and most individuals. This would suggest that a relative definition might be more productive (by avoiding fewer problems). But that conclusion is just the start of the task of trying to establish a definition.

REFERENCES

(1) B Mussolini *The Doctrine of Fascism* in *Social and Political Philosophy*, edited by J Somerville and R Santoni, Anchor Books, 1963, p. 426

(2) J S Mill *On Liberty*, in *Utilitarianism, Liberty, Representative Government*, J M Dent, 1910, p. 75

(3) *New Scientist*, 3 December 2005, p. 93

(4) Figures taken from *Pocket World in Figures 2006 Edition*, Profile Books, 2005, pp. 78–84

2
THE CONTINUUM OF CHOICE

In virtually every situation in which we find ourselves, we have a choice of some sort. Some of the situations might not look as if there is a choice, because we don't experience it as one which allows us to choose. For example 'Shall I get up this morning or not?' isn't normally a question that we ask ourselves on a normal school or college day. We just get up. But the question needs an answer.

Shall I get up this morning or not?

Yes————————————————No

But even with this question, there's something of a restriction of options going on. The simple Yes/No continuum could be unpacked into a series of answers.

Yes——Yes, but not for another half-hour——Yes, but not for another hour——
and so on

In that we are talking of a continuum of choice, we can see that choice normally involves much more than simple *x/not-x* options. If we are looking at issues of fact, then *x/not-x* options are much more likely. For example, the question

Is the diameter of the Earth 12,753 km?

has only one answer: 'Yes'. (Of course, with the understanding that this figure is likely to be a rounded-up or -down figure.)

Questions of judgement can also have simple Yes/No options.

Is Arsenal the greatest football team in England?

I might say 'yes' and you might say 'no'. (I am more likely to say 'it depends what you mean by "greatest"'.)

But questions of choice normally offer the scope for there to be a range of answers. This is especially so when we are looking at questions which have the form 'What should we do about *x*?' Some examples follow.

What should we do about football hooliganism?
What should we do about violent computer games?
What should we do about the lack of respect shown in our society?

With these sorts of questions, we have a range of responses.

What should we do about football hooliganism?

What we can do is just think of a number of possible responses.

- Ban from football matches all those who have ever been involved in football hooliganism.

- Increase the penalties for conviction for football hooliganism (including banning from any football ground).

- Penalise clubs whose supporters are involved in hooliganism (for example, by fining them).

- Increase the level of policing in and around football grounds where hooliganism is a problem.

- Recognise that football hooliganism is not a major problem with most football fans.

- Make those football clubs that have problems with football hooligans play at least some of their matches behind closed doors.

- Ban the consumption of alcohol in and near football grounds.

What we can see is that the question has a number of possible answers. Many of the answers are such that they don't rule out others as well. For example, we could both ban those who've been involved in hooliganism and penalise their clubs. This list of possible responses is not exhaustive, but it shows that questions like this cannot be answered by simple 'either do *x* or not-*x*'. This latter approach is beloved of a certain British newspaper which sees complex issues in very simple terms. Its shrill front page headlines present problems such as crime, poverty, and paying for pensions as 'Do *X* or encourage disaster/catastrophe/anarchy …'

What you will see from our list of possible responses to football hooliganism is not only that difficult issues cannot be solved by simple false dilemmas, but also that some of the responses can be ranked according to their severity. In other words, it's not a question of

X or catastrophe, but of a series of measures, each of which adds something. The previous list has been re-ordered to show this.

- Recognise that football hooliganism is not a major problem with most football fans.

- Increase the level of policing in and around football grounds where hooliganism is a problem.

- Ban the consumption of alcohol in and near football grounds.

- Ban from football matches all those who have ever been involved in football hooliganism.

- Increase the penalties for conviction for football hooliganism (including banning from any football ground).

- Make those football clubs that have problems with football hooligans play at least some of their matches behind closed doors.

What we have now is a series of answers to the problem each of which becomes more severe as we go down the list. Of course, there might be some disagreement on the degree of severity (for example, is the third less severe than the fourth?), but we get from this an idea of how a range of responses can be ranked.

We'll now look at one of the other questions.

What should we do about violent computer games?

The problem that the question is concerned with is normally the suggestion that these computer games can make people violent. We'll take the question to mean that, although it would be reasonable to ask the source of the question what they mean by it. Mischievously, we could treat the question as having other meanings such as 'What should we do to make violent games more available to all?' or 'What should we do about making violent games more realistic?'.

We'll try to construct a continuum of responses to the question, taking its meaning to refer to violent computer games making people violent. Because we're constructing a continuum, we're going to try to put together a range of responses which shows that, with each response, we've increased its severity.

We often think that 'doing nothing' is the starting point of such a continuum. However, it is often not the least severe response. In this particular case, a starting point could be

- encourage people to play violent computer games in the hope of reducing the chances of them being violent themselves. (A)

(The response has been labelled (A) so that we can identify it on the continuum that we're constructing.)

As you can see, this is going beyond doing nothing, in that it's actually seeing these games as having a potentially beneficial effect. We could make 'doing nothing' as the next response (B).

From there, we would expect that responses will add a degree of severity.

- Commission further research in order to demonstrate any effects of violent computer games. (C)

Though this doesn't look very severe, it is a step up from 'doing nothing'. The next response takes action against violent games a stage further.

- Encourage parents to exercise control over their children by monitoring what games they play. (D)

As you can see, it is not especially severe in that it does no more than recommend that we 'encourage' parents to control what games their children are playing. The next response goes beyond encouragement.

- Restrict the sales of the most violent computer games only to those aged 18 or over. (E)

This recommendation is obviously more severe in terms of action than any of the previous ones. It is concerned with actively reducing the availability of violent games. The next one goes even further.

- Restrict the sales of all computer games in which violence is portrayed only to those aged 18 or over. (F)

As we move to the opposite end of the continuum from encouraging people to play violent games, we find recommendations in which access to these games is getting more and more limited.

- Ban all computer games for which there is any evidence linking them with violent behaviour. (G)

We could, of course, go a stage further.

- Ban all computer games in which the violence is more than 'mild'. (H)

The continuum could be further extended.

- Ban all computer games in which there is any violence. (I)

If we were to create a continuum of choice, we would put it together as a horizontal line, showing the move from (A) to (I).

A———B———C———D———E———F———G———H———I

You could try to think of other entries that we put on this continuum of choice. An obvious one would be (J): Ban all computer games. Another one could be between (F) and (G): Restrict the sales of all computer games in which violence is portrayed only to those aged 25 or over.

ACTIVITY 1

In 2005, there was a great deal of talk about the need to do something about the debt owed by developing countries. The call was to 'make poverty history'. However, the subject is much more complicated than this slogan would suggest. What does it mean anyway?

A good starting point is to consider why the term 'poverty' is problematic to define. Explain why this is so.

ACTIVITY 2

Construct a continuum of choice showing a range of different responses to the question 'What should we do about the problem of debt owed by developing countries?'

ACTIVITY 1: COMMENTARY

The word 'poverty' has caused definitional problems for a long time. The importance of being able to deal with these definitional problems comes from various attempts to measure its extent or to reduce it. Of course, reducing it requires that we have a measure of what we're reducing.

Some of you will be familiar with some of the attempts to define poverty over the past hundred or so years. One of the most famous attempts to do this was that by Seebohm Rowntree (1871–1954). He wanted to find out the number of people living in poverty and so needed a definition.

His initial use of a measure of 'absolute' poverty gives us one way of seeking to deal with the problems of definition. If we take 'absolute' poverty to refer to a level of income which is insufficient for basic needs (food and shelter are the obvious ones), then we have something to work with. But you can immediately see that you have come up against the problematic nature via another route.

- What counts as basic food needs? Are we talking about starvation? Poor nutrition?

- What counts as basic needs of shelter? Are we talking about homelessness? Poor quality housing with few, if any, facilities?

Thus, if we are being encouraged to 'make poverty history', we need to know what we are making history. Is it starvation, malnutrition, lack of shelter, poor shelter, a combination of these, or what?

Rowntree's use of the notion of 'relative' poverty in later surveys that he carried out was an attempt to place poverty within a social context. The fact that someone isn't starving doesn't mean that they're not poor. This brings us to the problematic area of what counts as poverty in terms of what people expect to have in any society at a given time. We expect not only adequate food and shelter, but also things like TV, fridges, washing machines, and so on. Given that 98.8 per cent of UK households have at least one colour TV set, it is not surprising that a household without one (apart from out of choice) would experience (and be seen as being in a state of) deprivation. When we look at Nigeria, we find only 51.6 per cent of households having a colour TV, so the absence of one would not necessarily be seen as or experienced as deprivation.

Thus the definition of poverty is problematic because its content will change from place to place and from time to time. Even within a society at any one time, poverty will be seen in different ways. An 85 year-old in the UK today will not necessarily experience the lack of certain possessions as evidence of their poverty: computers, mobile phones, even cars. An 18 year-old, however, would probably see the absence of these as evidence of poverty.

When we read that Zimbabwe has the lowest quality of life of any country in the world[1], we don't know how many in that country are poor and how many aren't. President Mugabe and many of his close supporters won't be poor, but the 700,000 people that his government made homeless are likely to fall into some sort of definition of poverty.

We can, in this way, make the distinction between private and public poverty. When we talk about countries like Niger and Sudan being 'poor', we are making reference to those (admittedly large numbers) who are poor (by whatever standard we use). When we talk about the UK being a rich country, we are not making reference to the 12 million people classified as being poor.

Another aspect of the definition of poverty that you might have raised is that of whether poverty is something objective or subjective. When we say that 12 million people are poor in the UK (about one fifth of the population), do we mean that 12 million *are* poor or *feel* poor or both. We actually mean that 12 million are living on income (after council tax, rent or mortgage, and water charges have been deducted) that is 60 per cent or less of the average household income. (In 2003–04, this was £260 per week for two adults living with two children or £180 for one adult with two children.)[2] Do those income levels mean that those people who are at them feel poor? Does it mean that people above them don't? What about an income level that that is 65 per cent of average income: do these people not feel poor?

So your answer to this activity should have included at least some of the following.

Poverty is problematic to define because

- the content of its definition changes over time;
- the content of its definition changes from place to place;
- the content of its definition has different meaning depending on the focus: country, groups, families, individuals;
- it could have both an objective and a subjective meaning.

ACTIVITY 2: COMMENTARY

There are different ways that you could have approached this task. You could just come up with a number of responses and worry about their position on a continuum later. Alternatively, you could think of possible positions at the extremes of the continuum, and then try to fill in the stages in between.

We'll do it the first way and see how it works. (If you did it the other way, the outcome should still be similar.)

What should we do about the problem of debt owed by developing countries?

(A)   Enforce payment of the debt.

(B)   Enforce payment of only part of the debt.

(C)   Treat different countries differently.

(D)   Cancel the debt, with conditions for all countries.

(E)   Cancel the debt, with conditions for some countries.

(F)   Enforce payment of the debt, with sanctions to be applied if payments not made.

(G)   Make payment of the debt easier by extending the repayment period.

(H)   Cancel the debt, and provide financial help.

You might have had some of these (and some more). If we order them into a continuum, we are looking for one that shows, at the very least, a range from 'cancel the debt' to 'enforce the debt'. Taking the above list, we can see that the continuum goes further than each of these in both directions.

A suggested continuum, using the above responses, could be as follows.

F———A———B———G———C———D———E———H

We could construct a continuum with different extreme positions. For example:

- If no payment made, and sanctions not effective, military intervention to be used to seize property as payment of debt. (beyond F)

- Cancel the debt, provide financial help, and provide other help, such as medical care, agricultural products, and so on.

This continuum shows that the slogan 'make poverty history' obscures the range of positions on the continuum of choice.

We will return to this continuum later.

REFERENCES

(1) *The Economist Pocket World in Figures*, 2006 edition, Profile Books, 2005, p. 89

(2) 'Monitoring Poverty and Social Exclusion', New Policy Initiative, 2005 (www.poverty.org.uk/summary/key_facts.htm)

3
THE CRITERIA OF CHOICE

Having looked at what is involved in putting together a continuum of choice, we are now in a position to begin the task of seeing how we could begin to make decisions between the choices. The continuum of choice has the purpose of showing us what choices are available, but doesn't provide a means by which we could decide which choices are better than others. For this next step, we need criteria to help us.

WHAT DO WE MEAN BY 'CRITERIA OF CHOICE'?

The word 'criteria' is the plural of 'criterion'. We are using the word in its conventional way as referring to 'standard by which something can be judged'. It has the same Greek origin as the word 'critic' (someone who judges) and therefore, of course, 'critical'.

If we are searching for criteria of choice, we are then looking for ways by which we make judgements about choices. Having looked at how we create a continuum of choice, we want to now look at what criteria will help us to make these judgements.

Let's look again at the continuum of choice we created for the question 'What should we do about violent computer games?'

(A) Encourage people to play violent computer games in the hope of reducing the chances of them being violent themselves.

(B) Do nothing about the problem of violent computer games.

(C) Commission further research in order to demonstrate any effects of violent computer games.

(D) Encourage parents to exercise control over their children by monitoring what games they play.

(E) Restrict the sales of the most violent computer games only to those aged 18 or over.

(F) Restrict the sales of all computer games in which violence is portrayed only to those aged 18 or over.

(G)   Ban all computer games for which there is any evidence linking them with violent behaviour.

(H)   Ban all computer games in which the violence is more than 'mild'.

(I)   Ban all computer games in which there is any violence.

We need to look for criteria that will help us to choose the better option from this continuum.

An obvious criterion in this case is that of 'effectiveness'. In looking down the list (or across the continuum), we would have to say that, if the violence of computer games is a problem, we need to consider what would be the more effective solution. If we apply this, then at one level, clearly (I) is the most effective. But the position is likely to be more complicated than that. For one thing, we need to be clear about what we mean by 'violence'. This is a good example of the problem of definition that we looked at in Chapter 1. Why is 'violence' problematic for definition?

- There are different levels of what might count as 'violence'.

- There are different contexts for 'violence'.

- What might be seen as violent by one person/group of people might not be seen as violent by another.

In relation to computer games, these problems translate into specific issues.

- Can we lump together everything from *Toy Story* to *Resident Evil 4*, *Grand Theft Auto: San Andreas*, *God of War*, and *Manhunt* as all similarly violent? More specifically, is watching Buzz Lightyear zapping other toys with his laser gun, and watching prisoners burnt alive and victims torn in half the same thing: violence?

- Some contexts for violence might make it more justifiable. The obvious example would be games in which actions undertaken in war can be justified because of the context of war. In the game *Battlefield: 1942*, you would expect there to be shooting and shelling (and therefore death and injury), because World War II battles had both of them. But, in the game *Resident Evil 4*, can we similarly justify seeing a woman pinned to a wall by a pitchfork through her face as a necessary part of a fictitious account of the attempt to rescue the kidnapped daughter of the US President?

- The World Health Organisation (WHO) defines violence as 'The intentional use of physical force or power, threatened or actual, against oneself, another person or against a group or community, that either results in or has a likelihood of resulting in injury, death, psychological harm, mal-treatment or deprivation.'[1] Is this something that everyone would agree on? When the TV series *Rome* was screened, the scenes of violence (including crucifixion and rape) had to be removed from the version that was shown in Italy but not that which was shown in the UK.

- If we play a space-invaders game, are our attempts at destruction of alien spacecraft examples of violence? Not normally, in that references to violence are normally when humans (and some animals) are involved. Thus the Entertainment Software Rating Board (ESRB) that controls the rating of games in the UK is tolerant of cartoon and fantasy violence. It defines violence as 'aggressive conflict'. (If I were to produce a game in which marauding humans kill peace-loving, gentle, Nature-loving aliens on some distant planet, could this be acceptably non-violent?)

As we can see, the definition and perception of violence are important considerations in clarifying the choices that are available. But, even if we can solve the problem of what counts as a 'violent' computer game, we need to consider further what the criterion of effectiveness tells us about the question.

Each of the steps along the continuum has to be judged in terms of the extent to which it would solve the problem of violent computer games. If, as we have assumed, the problem is that those who play them have a higher risk of being violent in real life (such that the games have *caused* this higher risk), then the criterion of effectiveness could include measures which reduce this risk. The application of the criterion to test this will require that we look at evidence. But, if we look at (G) on the continuum, what seems like a reasonable recommendation at one level is problematic at another. (G) would allow violent computer games to be sold unless and until evidence could be provided that they caused violent behaviour. This is a problem in that, by then, the violent behaviour has been caused, at least with some individuals.

But there is another aspect of effectiveness that can be considered. This is the issue of **practicability**. In other words, to what extent could the steps on the continuum be carried out?

Look at (E) and (F).

- Restrict the sales of the most violent computer games only to those aged 18 or over. (E)

- Restrict the sales of all computer games in which violence is portrayed only to those aged 18 or over. (F)

What problem might there be for effectiveness because of practicability?

- Even if the games are sold only to those aged 18 or over, this does not mean that those under 18 will not be able to play them. (They could be bought by those who are 18 or over on behalf of younger people. Those under 18 could use them in their own homes.)

Look at (D).

- Encourage parents to exercise control over their children by monitoring what games they play. (D)

What problems might there be for effectiveness because of practicability?

- How could this be enforced?
- What does 'encourage' mean?

Look at (A).

- Encourage people to play violent computer games in the hope of reducing the chances of them being violent themselves. (A)

The same problems appear as with (D).

When we look at evidence regarding the issue of effectiveness, we will be able to see further how this criterion works in relation to the question.

A further criterion that will be useful is that of the law. If we're looking at recommendations that seek to 'restrict' or 'ban', then we need to know if these are choices that the law allows.

In the UK, there is a classification system for video games. The ESRB divides games into six categories. In terms of violence, the categories work as follows:

- EC (Early Childhood) – no inappropriate material
- E (Everyone) – might contain minimal cartoon, fantasy, or mild violence
- E10+ (Everyone 10 and older) – might contain more cartoon, fantasy, or mild violence
- T (Teen = suitable for 13 or over) – might contain violence, minimal blood
- M (Mature = suitable for 17 or older) – might contain intense violence, blood and gore

- AO (Adults Only = suitable only for 18 or over) – might include prolonged scenes of intense violence

Having provided the classification, the ESRB then relies on retailers to ensure that games are not sold inappropriately. In one case, WH Smith was fined for selling a magazine *PC Zone* which had a cover-mounted CD-Rom which contained a demo version of the game *Kingpin*. The game included scenes in which characters were clubbed, shot, and dismembered. WH Smith blamed the publishers of the magazine (who argued that the game was not excessively violent) but, by selling the magazine without restriction, WH Smith was found responsible.

We can see then that the application of the law can in some cases allow some of the options of the continuum to be used. However, if we look at the situation in the US, things get more complicated. There attempts to make sales of violent games to those under 18 illegal, have run into problems with the courts. A Californian law on this was blocked by a judge, as were similar laws in other states. Part of the case against these laws is that they violate the right to free speech. It is interesting to note that the judge ruled against the law, even if it could ever be shown that the games cause violent behaviour.

In the US context, then, the application of the criterion of the law would make many of the positions on the continuum unworkable (all from (E) to (I)).

We have so far looked at two criteria in relation to the continuum of choice regarding the question: *What should we do about violent computer games?* We have considered effectiveness (including practicability) and the law. Are there others that would be relevant?

- **Cost?** This is often a criterion that you'll find is relevant in examining positions on a continuum of choice. In that we're trying to look at how we can make decisions, the cost of particular proposals is normally an important consideration. We won't look at this here, but will meet it again later.

- **Public opinion?** Again, this is a criterion that's often very relevant. If we want to recommend one course of action rather than another, we might have to consider what public opinion is on the matter. In this case, for example, public opinion might favour putting the responsibility on parents to ensure that their children don't play unsuitable games rather than see the problem as one of banning games.

As we can see, criteria of choice are developed which have relevance to the question being answered. Some criteria are likely to appear in relation to most questions, whilst others will be very specific to the particular question being considered.

In order to take the task further, we would normally (as in most Critical Thinking tasks) look for **evidence**.

ACTIVITY 1

Read the article 'Bloodlust at the click of a mouse' Consider how any of the article could be used to inform decision-making about our continuum of choice about violent computer games.

Bloodlust at the click of a mouse [2]

The evidence is now out there that violent computer games desensitise young minds.

"CONTAINS FREQUENT strong bloody violence," reads the proud boast for 50 Cent: Bulletproof, one of the computer games that made popular gifts over the festive season. This one comes with a certificate 18 to indicate it is not suitable for children, but that will not have stopped any number of youngsters from sampling its delights. They will also have been enjoying Grand Theft Auto: San Andreas, *a witty number in which bonuses can be earned for killing prostitutes.*

In theory, retailers should not sell such games to those under the age of 18. That is hardly an obstacle: online shopping does away with that barrier. The nation's biggest grocer, Tesco, happily purveys the aforementioned games, along with God of War, *in which prisoners are burnt alive and victims torn in half, at its online store. Placing an order is taken to be an assurance that the buyer is over 18.*

Online retailers are such trusting sorts.

Juniors, however, do not have to resort to subterfuge to get their hands on games like these. A recent scare story reported how a boy of 11 collapsed unconscious while playing Resident Evil 4 *on his games console. It was a Christmas present, despite being rated 15, and despite including gory episodes such as a woman being pinned to a wall with the pitchfork through her face.*

Such incidents seem rare but what does cause concern is whether exposure to all this virtual violence does encourage violent behaviour in the real world. Most research has indicated that this is not necessarily so but that those who choose to play violent games are a self-selecting bunch who might already be more inclined towards violence.

This was part of the reason why the only attempt by the British Board of Film Classification to refuse a certificate to a game was overturned on appeal. The BBFC, whose members must be of a pretty unshockable disposition, thought that Carmageddon went a step too far and that it could be harmful. But the distributors went to the appeals tribunal and the game went on sale with an 18 certificate.

That was in the mid-1990s and there has not been any cause for a distributor to appeal since. Even the nastiest of games has been granted an 18 certificate and become available to those who like to spend hours fighting virtual battles.

Whatever previous research has determined, it is hard to believe that prolonged exposure to such horrors does not breed some nasty ideas in the more impressionable of minds. The instances in which youngsters have gone out and committed murders akin to those they have watched are mercifully rare, although there have been a few notorious cases. But instinct suggests that bloodlust cultivated on a computer screen might at least have a desensitising effect, even if it does not drive the player to go out and kill a few prostitutes.

Now some new research seems to back up that view. Scientists at the University of Missouri-Columbia have determined that regular players of violent games suffer reduction in a type of brain activity called the P300 response, which reflects the emotional impact of an image on the viewer. The reaction of gamers to violent images was muted, suggesting that they were desensitised to brutality. They were also found more likely to behave aggressively, although we should be reassured that, apparently, they had a normally sympathetic reaction to photographs of dead animals or ill children. We are not told whether they would give up their seat on the train to elderly people or kick them out of the way.

The BBFC is not, however, rushing to rethink its policies and one can see why. The research was conducted on just 39 experienced game players. There would need to be something very much more conclusive before a move towards banning certain games began to gather support. Such a move would meet fierce opposition from the games industry, which is now a colossal international business and one in which Britain is a leading player.

Yet not even the BBFC is sanguine about the way in which the market works. For children to be spending large parts of their day exposed to non-stop violence cannot be the best start in life. Apart from pandering to their less attractive traits, it will also contribute to making them fat. But the regulators of violence and pornography – there's a dose of that in computer games too – cannot kick the children off their chairs and into the garden. That is the job of parents.

It is difficult to know what children are doing when they sit in front of the computer. There has been panic that they could be making undesirable assignations through internet chat rooms but they might just as easily be stoking up on violence through computer games. It should not be beyond modern technology to create devices so that parents could prevent computers from accepting games deemed unsuitable for children.

Sad to relate, the average age of the computer game player is 28. If adults choose to spend their free time experiencing Resident Evil, *perhaps we should not try to stand in their way. But we might as well have a go at preventing children from being exposed to too much nastiness too early in their lives.*

© Patience Wheatcroft., NI Syndication Limited, January 2006

Hopefully, you can see that the process we have been through so far has been useful in clarifying the issues to do with making a decision. We have done four significant things.

- We have clarified problems of definition. What do we mean by a 'violent' computer game?

- We have constructed a continuum of choice showing a wide range of options as responses to the question about violent computer games.

- We have considered criteria that would be useful in choosing between the options on the continuum.

- In Activity 1, we have looked at an argument on this subject. In doing so, we evaluated the claims that were being made. We did this both in order to examine the meaning of the evidence used and to consider what significance it has for the options on our continuum of choice.

However, though we have made considerable progress, we still have not yet made a decision. We will take further steps towards making a decision in the next section.

But, before we do, it will be useful to show the process so far in diagrammatic form.

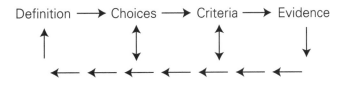

Definition ⟶ Choices ⟶ Criteria ⟶ Evidence

This shows how we have moved through the different stages. But it does not capture the fact that the process has been in more than one direction. For example, when considering the evidence, we found that it suggested more choices. Thus we need to show the process as a much more interactive one.

This interactive model shows that the decision-making process we have been putting together has the virtue of 'feedback'. We can revisit any stage of the process in the light of what we consider at subsequent stages.

We will add to this model as we progress through the following sections.

ACTIVITY 1: COMMENTARY

- The second paragraph has some useful information on the problem of enforcing (E) and (F). On-line shopping makes it much more difficult for retailers to ensure that only those 18 or over buy products.

- The third paragraph could be used to reinforce the significance of (D), although it could also be used to show again how restriction of sales in shops has little significance if the violent computer games are bought for young people by others.

  Interestingly, the case referred to of the 11 year-old boy collapsing unconscious is a good example of how two things are conflated such that meaning or significance is distorted. The story of the 11 year-old boy was headlined in *The Daily Mail* as 'Boy has fit playing violent computer game'. The strong suggestion of a causal link is very clear. However, much of the accompanying article was showing that epilepsy can be triggered by the flickering of images on the screen. High levels of screen brightness and contrast which cause flickering seem to be the main problem. In other words, this example is something of a red herring in that 'Boy has fit playing computer game' is more the point of the story.

- The fourth paragraph presents the position that the relationship between playing violent games and being violent should be seen in reverse. It serves to remind us that *post hoc* relationships can often usefully be considered in this way. If the relationship can be reversed in this case, then the issue of what should be done about violent games becomes a very different one. It would lend support to (B). Alternatively, it could be used to produce a new recommendation: 'Restrict the sales of violent computer games to those who do not show prior signs of aggressive tendencies.' Of course, this has too many problems to implement, but it would be legitimate to place it on the continuum of choice. (It would have to placed at the same point as either (E) or (F), depending on which of these is seen as the most relevant.)

- The fifth paragraph gives us useful information which can be used in relation to (G), (H), and (I). Given the problems that have been found in trying to ban certain games, these recommendations seem unworkable.

- The sixth paragraph is interesting from a Critical Thinking perspective. 'Whatever previous research has determined, it is hard to believe that prolonged exposure to such horrors does not breed some nasty ideas in the more impressionable of minds.' It is an example where somebody rejects evidence because it just doesn't seem to fit with what they believe. Though it can be useful to be sceptical of evidence, one cannot dismiss it entirely without counter-evidence. The author then refers to 'a few notorious cases' but there is a dispute over these. Perhaps the most famous was the suggested linking of the killing of the two-year-old James Bulger in 1993. The two ten-year-olds who killed him were supposed to have been influenced by the film *Child's Play 3*. The newspaper *The Sun* organised a public burning of the film. However, there was absolutely no evidence to link the film with the killing (for example, the police completely rejected the link). In another case, the same film was linked with the killing of a teenager. Again the evidence of such a link was not found. The linking of the Hungerford killings in 1987 with the Rambo film *First Blood* was similarly lacking in evidence. Perhaps most importantly, there was no evidence that the killer Michael Ryan had ever seen the film.

  In this way Patience Wheatcroft's reference to 'a few notorious cases' runs the risk of repeating earlier unsubstantiated links between violent media and violent behaviour.

  Of course, even if you didn't know about these cases (and thus whether or not they were good examples), you would still gain credit for making the general point that it is difficult to generalise from 'a few notorious cases'.

- Wheatcroft's claim that 'instinct suggests that bloodlust cultivated on a computer screen might at least have a desensitising effect' is reinforced by research described in paragraph seven. This research would be relevant to (C), (G), (H), and (I). In that we don't know anything about the age of the people in the study, the research doesn't enable us to use it to support any of the positions that refer to age. If we wanted to ask questions about the significance of the research, we would need to know such things as what criteria were used to define 'aggressively' and the relevance of a 'muted' reaction to 'violent images'. To what extent was it muted? Does a muted response translate into a greater willingness to be aggressive? To what extent did the players already have muted reactions prior to playing these games?

The last sentence of this paragraph has a distinctly un-Critical Thinking look to it. One obvious response to it is that it is an example of restriction of options: there are behaviours in between these two extremes. Another one is that this is an example of what we can describe as 'rhetoric' (see pages 151–152). It is an attempt to be persuasive that is not to do with a rigorous evaluation of the research. At one important level, this sentence does nothing at all in the argument.

- Paragraph eight provides useful evaluation of the research referred to in the previous paragraph. The smallness of the sample used is a notable weakness in the evidence. The reference to 'experienced game players' is another point. (In the previous paragraph they are referred to as 'regular players'.) Any recommendations about what should be done about violent computer games would have to take this limitation on board. What sort of effect do these games have on occasional players? Obviously, then, these considerations reinforce recommendation (C).

The second part of this paragraph is relevant to recommendations (G), (H), and (I). The author gives a reason why banning games would be very difficult.

- The ninth paragraph is relevant to recommendation (D). This could be used to support an argument that the role of parents has to be seen as central to the problem of what to do about violent computer games. The point that 'spending large parts of their day exposed to non-stop violence … will contribute to making (children) fat' is very much a red herring here. The obvious response is that if children spend 'large parts of their day' playing *any* computer game (however non-violent), the same point presumably applies. Playing violent games in itself does not make us fat.

- Paragraph ten is another good example of rhetoric. The phrase 'stoking up on violence through computer games' means little, though its purpose is to alarm us. However, the paragraph contains something useful for recommendation (D). Wheatcroft argues that there should be a way by which parents could prevent their computers being able to play unsuitable games.

This is a very useful point and could be used to produce a new recommendation. This could be 'Develop the technology to allow parents to restrict the type of games that can be played on their home computers.' We could put this between (D) and (E). It is a good example where evidence can inform decision-making.

Interestingly, this is an area where there is already some relevant development. Nintendo have announced that their new machine 'Revolution' contains a device enabling anyone (such as a parent) to stop the console from playing certain games. The system works by recognising age-restricted games. Sony's Playstation 3 and Microsoft's Xbox 360 offer the same facility.

* The final paragraph gives us evidence that weakens the significance of recommendations (D), (E), and (F). If the average age of computer game players is 28, then these recommendations might miss much of the point. You would need to consider whether this evidence makes our question of what we should do about violent computer games a less significant one. Perhaps the question needs to be adjusted to focus only on children.

However, these considerations work on the assumption that any undesirable effects of violent games were relevant only to children and young people. Perhaps older people are affected in the same way. Perhaps it is even more of a problem with older people in that they might have more opportunities to put their heightened aggressive tendencies to bad use.

Why does Wheatcroft say that it is 'sad to relate' that the average age is 28? Is the playing of computer games seen as something that only children should be doing? Given that she is concerned in the rest of the article with the problem of children playing violent games, would the average age figure not be something that she should welcome?

There is, however, another point. The average age refers to the 'computer game player'. We do not know if the average age of players of violent games is different.

Wheatcroft's reference to this average age is coupled with her point that if adults want to play violent games, 'perhaps we should not try to stand in their way.' This point supports recommendation (B).

REFERENCES

(1) 'World Report on Violence and Health', World Health Organisation, 2002

(2) *The Times*, 13th January 2006

4

IDENTIFYING DILEMMAS

In the Introduction to Part 1, we considered the point that decisions about problems have to be made all the time. We specifically raised the point that governments are faced with such decisions. Furthermore we considered the problem that governments face in making decisions. They are always going to be faced with the problem that, whatever they do, some people are going to be upset. For example, the proposal to ban smoking in all pubs and clubs pleases some people and angers others.

Peter Hollins, director-general of the British Heart Foundation:

> '(This) is a landmark victory for the public health of this country, which will save the lives of many people across the UK.'

> 'If the people of Rotherham want to smoke themselves to death, what business is it of the people of London?'
>
> Simon Jenkins, The Guardian, February 15th 2006.

If we approach this subject as a false dilemma, and propose that smoking should be banned in some pubs and clubs but not all of them, then we do not necessarily make the decision-making less of a problem. This is what the Government proposed in 2005, but it still managed to upset many people including the Chief Medical Officer (who threatened to resign because there wasn't a complete ban).

Though it is unlikely that any decision that affects the public will not be controversial in some way, the fact that decisions have to be made reinforces our interest in the role of Critical Thinking in informing the decision-making process.

Unit 3's title is the 'resolution of dilemmas'. Thus there are two things that we need to consider.

- What do we mean by a 'dilemma'?
- How do we resolve one?

WHAT DO WE MEAN BY A 'DILEMMA'?

The New Oxford Dictionary of English gives the following definitions.

A situation in which a difficult choice has to be made between two or more alternatives, especially ones that are equally undesirable
A difficult situation or problem

The Oxford Dictionary stresses that the second definition, though it has been in use since the 17th century is one that is not used commonly. The first one, however, contains the meaning that we are looking for. A very familiar usage (especially with philosophers) is that a dilemma is always between two equally undesirable alternatives.

There is a children's book called *Would You Rather?* which provides lots of such dilemmas. The reader is given lots of options to choose from, each of which has a problem (an often big one). (Examples include the options of spider stew or slug dumplings and being lost at sea or in the desert.)

Very compelling dilemmas would be between telling the truth or betraying someone, when either choice would cause someone to suffer. Being under torture faced with this choice would be an extreme example. Another extreme one would be that faced by people adrift in a boat when the survival of many of them would require the death of some (so who should die?).

There is an exercise called 'the prisoners' dilemma' in which two prisoners have to calculate whether or not to betray the other in order to gain an advantage for themselves. This is supposed to be a good example of how one should make a decision based on both self-interest and a judgement of how you think someone else is going to behave. (Unfortunately, when I tried it on a group of prisoners, they couldn't see any dilemma because 'you don't grass on anyone'.)

So an obvious feature of a dilemma is a choice between at least two options. It is also a difficult choice. Shall I buy this birthday card or that one is a choice between at least two options. It might even be seen as being difficult. But the difficulty is at a fairly low level. In a recent publicity leaflet from Oxfam, having asked the question 'What was the last dilemma you faced?' they give examples such as 'stay in, go out?' They do this in order to show that such daily 'dilemmas' aren't that serious. The purpose is to contrast our easy lives with those of many people in the developing countries. The example given by Oxfam emphasises the difference between many of our dilemmas and theirs. It concerns Misgane Chloe in Ethiopia.

'I had two options for drinking water. If I was tired I would fetch the water three hours away, but this was not clean. If I had more energy I would go and fetch the cleaner water that was a five hour journey.'

When we are using dilemma to mean a difficult choice, we are using the term to refer to situations in which there is an ethical dimension to the choice. Choosing between birthday cards might be difficult but choosing one rather than the other has no obvious ethical consequence. We are looking at social, economic, or political decision-making in this Unit, but sometimes dilemmas of this type have individual dilemmas within them. The one faced by Misgane Chloe has a moral dimension in that her choice affected her eight children. Whether or not Oxfam can help people like her is linked to bigger dilemmas as to what solutions should be adopted at a national and international level.

So the question 'What should we do about *x*?' in this dilemmas unit is going to refer to issues where there is a range of responses and each response can be judged in terms of an ethical dimension.

For example, the issue of whether or not smoking should be allowed in public places has a range of responses each of which raises an ethical issue. The following are examples.

- Should we restrict the freedom of those who wish to smoke for the sake of those who don't?

- Should protecting the health of people be more important than giving them freedom of choice?

- Should smoking be allowed where the majority of people involved want it to be?

But, though important, these are questions rather than dilemmas. A dilemma, as we have seen, involves a choice between at least two options. If we wanted to see these questions as dilemmas, we would have to give alternative positions. The following shows how this could work.

- Should smoking be allowed where the majority of people involved want it to be or should the State enforce a smoking ban for the sake of people's health?

In this example, both options could be defended. With the first, we could appeal to the principle of democracy; with the second, we could appeal to the principle of protecting people from harm.

Going back to our earlier consideration of the problem of violent computer games, we had identified some criteria that would be relevant in deciding how we should decide what to do. One of these was public opinion. If we want to simply identify an issue with the violent games problem, we could use this criterion.

- Should public opinion be taken into account when dealing with violent computer games?

As before, there is no dilemma. There is just a question which identifies an issue. If we want to use the criterion of public opinion in a dilemma, we need to balance it with a different criterion. We could use another we identified earlier, that of the law.

- Should public opinion be taken into account when dealing with violent computer games or should we use the existing laws to deal with the problem?

In this version, we are faced with having to make a choice. Which criterion is the one that should best determine what we should do? In order to answer this question, we would look (critically, as always) at any evidence that we have available. But we are going to be doing something else too. We are going to use an ethical framework as part of our answer. Out of this process will come a recommendation as to how we should act, what we should do. As we already considered in the Introduction, we are here concerned with Critical Thinking as means of answering practical questions with practical answers. How should we act? We should do x.

An example of a practical question that needs answering is 'what should we do to increase the level of personal safety?' You can see how our method of decision-making could help us to answer this question.

- We need to look at how 'personal safety' can be defined.

- We need to construct a continuum of choice, showing a range of different options.

- We need to consider what criteria would be relevant in choosing between the positions on the continuum of choice.

- We need to look at evidence regarding each of the criteria.

At this stage, we have gone a long way in the process of moving towards a decision. The next step is to identify dilemmas. The following would be an example of one that would probably emerge from this process.

- Should we increase the level of surveillance of people (such as through CCTV and the frequent checking of identity through ID cards) in order to increase levels of personal safety or should we not sacrifice privacy for security?

If we concluded that increasing the level of surveillance was justified in order to increase personal safety, then our conclusion would have to be evaluated just like the conclusion of any argument. Is it in any way overdrawn?

To evaluate the conclusion in relation to the reasoning that had preceded it, we need to look at the evidence that is used and the handling of the issue of principle. We can question the conclusion via either route.

- Is the evidence relevant to the conclusion?

- Does the evidence have the significance it is given in the argument?

- Is there other evidence that ought to have been considered?

- Has the issue of privacy been balanced against other ethical considerations?

In that we have highlighted the importance of an ethical component to producing and evaluating decisions, the next chapter will address the question of how using an ethical framework can inform our decision-making.

ACTIVITY 1

In the Activity in Chapter 2 you looked at producing a continuum of choice in response to the campaign to 'make poverty history'. In Chapter 3 we looked at how we needed to use criteria in helping us to make decisions. In this Activity, you can apply what you learned there to the subject of debt-relief in developing countries.

Suggest criteria that could be useful in helping us to decide how to choose between positions on the continuum developed in Chapter 2. For each criterion you identify, provide an explanation of why it could be relevant.

You will find below various pieces of evidence. These provide statistical information which you will find useful in both thinking of relevant criteria and explaining their relevance.

For your benefit, the continuum of choice about debt-relief in poor countries is given again. It has been put into the order shown diagrammatically on page 23, with the two extreme positions added. We have numbered the options for ease of reference.
- If no payment made, and sanctions not effective, military intervention to be used to seize property as payment of debt. (1)
- Enforce payment of the debt, with sanctions to be applied if payments not made. (2)
- Enforce payment of the debt. (3)
- Enforce payment of only part of the debt. (4)
- Make payment of the debt easier by extending the repayment period. (5)
- Treat different countries differently. (6)

- Cancel the debt, with conditions for all countries. (7)
- Cancel the debt, with conditions for some countries. (8)
- Cancel the debt, and provide financial help. (9)
- Cancel the debt, provide financial help, and provide other help, such as medical care, agricultural products, and so on. (10)

EVIDENCE

USE OF AID

In Swaziland, King Mswati III spent £500,000 on eight Mercedes cars with gold-plated number plates. He also spent £8 million on palaces for his thirteen wives and £330,000 on his 36th birthday party. 700,000 people live in poverty (out of a population of 1.1 million), though the country received £15 million of aid in 2003. The UK gave £550,000 of this.

In Nigeria, £2.8 billion of aid was spent opening a steel factory in Ajaokuta. £1.1 billion was allegedly stolen by cronies of Sani Abacha, the late dictator, and £27 million went on the factory's upkeep. The factory produced nothing.[1]

HUMAN RIGHTS

If we look at the human rights record of many of the countries on the list of those that need economic help, we find that the record is normally poor.

For example

- Cameroon: very poor record, with claims of torture and death in police custody.

- Democratic Republic of Congo: very poor record, with unlawful killings, rape, torture, use of children as soldiers all widespread.

- Ethiopia: very poor record, with widespread arbitrary detentions and torture.

- Mauritania: poor record with slavery and forced labour being reported, and unfair trials and torture being widespread.

- Niger: poor record, with slavery widespread, and little press freedom.

Other countries, however, have a much better human rights record.

For example

- Benin: good record, though occasional harassment of journalists and arbitrary detention.

- Gambia: fair record, and the ban on political parties has been lifted.

- Mali: good, though some reports of arbitrary detention.

- Senegal: good record, with a president who is a supporter of reform and democracy.

- Sierra Leone: fair record, and war-crimes trials have started.[2]

Tanzania	20.83
Mozambique	19.46
Ethiopia	18.80
Kenya	13.65
Zambia	13.15
DR of Congo	13.09
Sudan	13.09
Uganda	12.15
Ghana	12.04
Ivory Coast	11.43

Top ten recipients of aid 1984-2003 in US$bn [3]

Tanzania	fair
Mozambique	good
Ethiopia	very poor
Kenya	poor
Zambia	poor
DR of Congo	very poor
Sudan	poor
Uganda	poor
Ghana	good
Ivory Coast	poor

Top ten recipients of aid and human rights record [4]

CORRUPTION

The extent of corruption in different countries might be difficult to establish. However, the following table shows the *perception* of corruption in different countries. It is based on reports from business people, academics, and people whose expertise is to analyse risk. They are looking for corruption amongst politicians and public officials. (There is likely, of course, to also be corruption within private businesses.)

Corruption perceptions index			
2004, 10 = least corrupt			
Lowest		Highest	
1 Finland	9.7	1 Bangladesh	1.5
2 New Zealand	9.6	Haiti	1.5
3 Denmark	9.5	3 Nigeria	1.6
Iceland	9.5	4 Chad	1.7
5 Singapore	9.3	Myanmar	1.7
6 Sweden	9.2	6 Azerbaijan	1.9
7 Switzerland	9.1	Paraguay	1.9
8 Norway	8.9	8 Angola	2.0
9 Australia	8.8	Congo	2.0
10 Netherlands	8.7	Côte d'Ivoire	2.0
11 United Kingdom	8.6	Georgia	2.0
12 Canada	8.5	Indonesia	2.0
13 Austria	8.4	Tajikistan	2.0
Luxembourg	8.4	Turkmenistan	2.0
15 Germany	8.2		

Corruption perceptions index [5]

LIVING STANDARDS

(GDP means Gross Domestic Product which refers to the sum of all output produced by economic activity within a country. It does not include any income from overseas.)

Lowest GDP per head $				
1	Burundi	90	11 Mozambique	230
	Ethiopia	90	Nepal	230
3	Congo	110	Niger	230
4	Liberia	130	14 Uganda	240
5	Malawi	140	15 Tajikistan	250
6	Guinea-Bissau	160	16 Gambia, The	280
	Sierra Leone	160	Tanzania	280
8	Eritrea	180	18 Bhutan	300
9	Rwanda	190	Cambodia	300
10	Afghanistan	200	Chad	300

Lowest GDP per head in $ [6]

The country with the highest GDP per head in the world is Luxembourg with $52,990; the US has $37,240; the UK (in at fifteenth) has $30,280.

Highest GDP per head $				
1	Luxembourg	52,990	36 Puerto Rico	17,420
2	Norway	49,080	37 Israel	17,220
3	Switzerland	44,460	38 Kuwait	16,700
4	Denmark	39,330	39 Bahamas	16,590
5	Ireland	38,430	40 Greece	15,650
6	United States	37,240	41 Martinique	15,560
7	Iceland	36,960	42 Cyprus	14,790
8	Bermuda	35,940	43 Portugal	14,640
9	Sweden	33,890	44 French Polynesia	14,190
10	Japan	33,680	45 Slovenia	14,130
11	Netherlands	31,770	46 South Korea	12,690
12	Austria	31,410	47 Taiwan	12,670
13	Finland	31,070	48 Malta	12,160
14	Cayman Islands	30,950	49 New Caledonia	11,920
15	United Kingdom	30,280	50 Netherlands Antilles	11,140
16	France	29,240	51 Bahrain	10,790
17	Belgium	29,170	52 Barbados	9,690
18	Germany	29,130	53 Saudi Arabia	8,870
19	Qatar	27,990	54 Czech Republic	8,790
20	Canada	27,190	55 Hungary	8,360
21	Australia	26,520	56 Trinidad & Tobago	8,010
22	Italy	25,580	57 Guadeloupe	7,950
23	United Arab Emirates	23,650	58 Oman	7,480
24	Hong Kong	22,380	59 Estonia	6,990
25	Virgin Islands	22,320	60 Croatia	6,540
26	Faroe Islands	21,600	61 Mexico	6,050
27	Singapore	21,490	62 Slovakia	6,040
28	New Zealand	20,400	63 Equatorial Guinea	5,900
	Spain	20,400	64 Réunion	5,750
30	Guam	19,750	65 Poland	5,430
31	Greenland	19,640	66 Lithuania	5,360
32	Aruba	18,940	67 Lebanon	5,040
33	Andorra	18,790	68 Latvia	4,770
34	Brunei	18,260	69 Chile	4,590
35	Macau	17,790	70 Gabon	4,510

Highest GDP per head in $ [6]

LIFE EXPECTANCY

Highest life expectancy			
Years, 2005–10			
1 Andorra	83.5	Guadeloupe	79.2
2 Japan	82.8	27 Aruba	79.1
3 Hong Kong	82.2	Luxembourg	79.1
4 Iceland	81.4	Malta	79.1
5 Switzerland	81.1	United Arab Emirates	79.1
6 Australia	81.0	31 Channel Islands	79.0
7 Sweden	80.8	Netherlands	79.0
8 Canada	80.7	United Kingdom	79.0
Macau	80.7	34 Costa Rica	78.8
10 Israel	80.6	35 Greece	78.7
11 Italy	80.6	36 Chile	78.6
12 Norway	80.2	Cuba	78.6
13 Spain	80.1	38 Ireland	78.5
14 Cayman Islands	80.0	39 South Korea	78.2
France	80.0	40 Portugal	77.9
16 New Zealand	79.8	United States	77.9
17 Austria	79.7	42 Bermuda[a]	77.8
18 Belgium	79.6	Denmark	77.8
19 Martinique	79.4	44 Kuwait	77.6
Singapore	79.4	45 Taiwan	77.3
21 Finland	79.3	46 Slovenia	77.2
Germany	79.3	47 Brunei	77.1
23 Virgin Islands	79.3	48 Netherlands Antilles	76.9
24 Cyprus	79.2	49 Puerto Rico	76.8
Faroe Islands	79.2	50 Barbados	76.4

Lowest life expectancy			
Years, 2005–10			
1 Swaziland	29.9	26 Ethiopia	48.5
2 Botswana	33.9	27 Somalia	48.8
3 Lesotho	34.3	28 Burkina Faso	49.3
4 Zimbabwe	37.3	Mali	49.3
5 Zambia	39.1	30 Kenya	50.3
6 Central African Rep	39.5	31 Uganda	52.1
7 Malawi	41.1	32 Gabon	53.3
8 Equatorial Guinea	41.5	33 Congo-Brazzaville	53.5
9 Mozambique	41.8	Haiti	53.5
10 Angola	41.9	35 Guinea	54.4
Sierra Leone	41.9	36 Mauritania	54.5
12 Liberia	42.5	37 Togo	55.8
13 South Africa	44.1	38 Benin	55.9
14 Nigeria	44.2	39 Eritrea	56.0
15 Chad	44.3	40 Madagascar	56.2
16 Rwanda	44.6	41 Laos	56.5
17 Congo	44.7	42 Sudan	56.9
18 Niger	45.4	43 Papua New Guinea	57.1
19 Guinea-Bissau	45.5	Senegal	57.1
20 Burundi	45.6	45 Gambia, The	57.7
21 Namibia	45.9	46 Cambodia	58.0
22 Côte d'Ivoire	46.2	47 Ghana	58.1
23 Cameroon	46.3	48 Iraq	61.0
24 Tanzania	46.6	49 Myanmar	61.8
25 Afghanistan	47.7	50 Yemen	62.7

Highest and lowest life expectancy [7]

LEVELS OF AID

(from a report by Oxfam[8])

'Between 1960-65, rich countries spent on average 0.48 per cent of their combined national incomes on aid. By 1980-85 they were spending just 0.34 per cent. By 2003, the average had dropped to 0.24 per cent.'

'... poor countries continue to pay out more to their creditors than they spend on essential public services. Low income countries paid $39 billion to service their debts in 2003, while they received only $27 billion in aid. As a result, countries such as Zambia spend more on debt servicing than they spend on education.'

'Rich countries can easily afford to deliver the necessary aid and debt relief. For rich countries, spending 0.7 per cent of their national income on aid is equal to a mere one-fifth of their expenditure on defence and one half of their expenditure on domestic farm subsidies.'

'Nor is 0.7 per cent very great when compared with the priorities of global consumers, who spend $33 billion each year on cosmetic and perfume – significantly more than the $20-25 billion required' (to meet poverty-reduction targets).

GIVERS AND RECEIVERS OF AID

Largest bilateral and multilateral donors

$m

1	United States	16,320	14	Denmark	1,748
2	Japan	8,880	15	Switzerland	1,299
3	France	7,253	16	Australia	1,219
4	Germany	6,784	17	Finland	558
5	United Kingdom	6,282	18	Austria	505
6	Netherlands	3,981	19	Ireland	504
7	Italy	2,433	20	South Korea	366
8	Sweden	2,400	21	Greece	362
9	Saudi Arabia	2,391	22	Portugal	320
10	Norway	2,042	23	Luxembourg	194
11	Canada	2,031	24	United Arab Emirates	188
12	Spain	1,961	25	New Zealand	165
13	Belgium	1,853	26	Kuwait	133

Largest recipients of bilateral and multilateral aid

$m

1	Congo	5,381	33	Mali	528
2	Iraq	2,265	34	Morocco	523
3	Vietnam	1,769	35	French Polynesia	519
4	Indonesia	1,743	36	Cambodia	508
5	Tanzania	1,669	37	Peru	500
6	Afghanistan	1,533	38	Angola	499
7	Ethiopia	1,504	39	Malawi	498
8	Bangladesh	1,393	40	Kenya	483
9	China	1,325	41	Nepal	467
10	Serbia & Montenegro	1,317	42	New Caledonia	454
11	Russia	1,255	43	Niger	453
12	Jordan	1,234	44	Burkina Faso	451
13	Poland	1,191	45	Senegal	450
14	Pakistan	1,068	46	Israel	440
15	Mozambique	1,033	47	Bulgaria	414
16	West Bank and Gaza	972	48	Honduras	389
17	Uganda	959	49	Lithuania	372
18	India	942	50	Albania	342
19	Bolivia	930	51	Rwanda	332
20	Ghana	907	52	Ukraine	323
21	Egypt	894	53	Nigeria	318
22	Cameroon	884	54	Eritrea	307
23	Nicaragua	833	55	Tunisia	306
24	Colombia	802	56	Laos	299
25	Philippines	737	57	Azerbaijan	297
26	Sri Lanka	672		Sierra Leone	297
27	South Africa	625	59	Brazil	296
28	Sudan	621	60	Benin	294
29	Romania	601	61	Kazakhstan	268
30	Zambia	560	62	Czech Republic	263
31	Bosnia	539	63	Côte d'Ivoire	252
	Madagascar	539	64	Hungary	248

Givers and receivers of aid (dollars) [9]

Largest bilateral and multilateral donors
% of GDP

1	Saudi Arabia	1.11	14	Germany	0.28
2	Norway	0.92	15	United Arab Emirates	0.26
3	Denmark	0.84	16	Australia	0.25
4	Luxembourg	0.81	17	Canada	0.24
5	Netherlands	0.80	18	New Zealand	0.23
6	Sweden	0.79		Spain	0.23
7	Belgium	0.60	20	Portugal	0.22
8	France	0.41	21	Greece	0.21
9	Ireland	0.39	22	Austria	0.20
	Switzerland	0.39		Japan	0.20
11	Finland	0.35	24	Iceland	0.17
12	United Kingdom	0.34		Italy	0.17
13	Kuwait	0.32	26	United States	0.15

Largest recipients of bilateral and multilateral aid
$ per head

1	French Polynesia	2,161		Zambia	55
2	New Caledonia	2,064	33	Bahrain	54
3	West Bank and Gaza	301		Laos	54
4	Jordan	239	35	Bulgaria	53
5	Serbia & Montenegro	161	36	Lebanon	51
6	Netherlands Antilles	158	37	Latvia	49
7	Nicaragua	156	38	Belize	48
8	Bosnia	131	39	Tanzania	47
9	Macedonia	114	40	Ghana	46
10	Albania	109		Malawi	46
11	Lithuania	107		Mali	46
12	Bolivia	106	43	Benin	45
13	Congo	104		Senegal	45
14	Mongolia	101	45	Equatorial Guinea	44
15	Guinea-Bissau	100		Lesotho	44
16	Iraq	94	47	Gambia, The	43
17	Mauritania	92	48	Georgia	42
18	Bhutan	91	49	Papua New Guinea	41
19	Armenia	81		Rwanda	41
20	Macau	75	51	Kirgizstan	40
21	Barbados	74		Niger	40
22	Namibia	73	53	Cambodia	39
23	Eritrea	71		Uganda	39
24	Israel	67	55	Angola	38
25	Estonia	62		Burkina Faso	38
	Fiji	62	57	Azerbaijan	36
27	Honduras	57	58	Sri Lanka	35
	Sierra Leone	57	59	Madagascar	33
29	Cameroon	56	60	Burundi	32
	Mozambique	56		Liberia	32
31	Afghanistan	55			

Givers and receivers of aid (percentage) [9]

CONDITIONS FOR RECEIPT OF AID

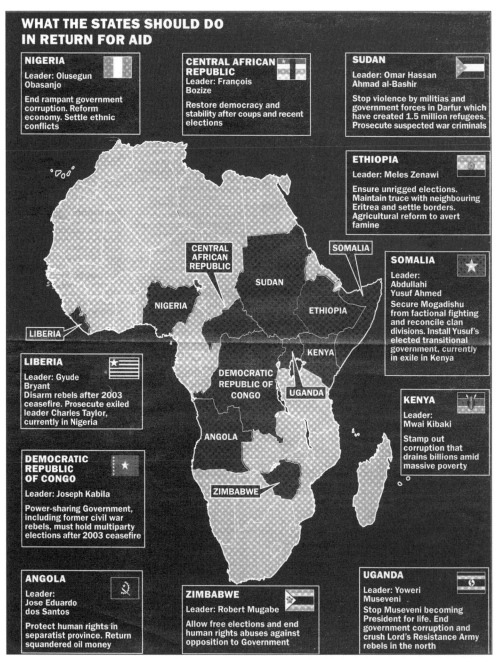

WHAT THE STATES SHOULD DO IN RETURN FOR AID

NIGERIA
Leader: Olusegun Obasanjo

End rampant government corruption. Reform economy. Settle ethnic conflicts

CENTRAL AFRICAN REPUBLIC
Leader: François Bozize

Restore democracy and stability after coups and recent elections

SUDAN
Leader: Omar Hassan Ahmad al-Bashir

Stop violence by militias and government forces in Darfur which have created 1.5 million refugees. Prosecute suspected war criminals

ETHIOPIA
Leader: Meles Zenawi

Ensure unrigged elections. Maintain truce with neighbouring Eritrea and settle borders. Agricultural reform to avert famine

SOMALIA
Leader: Abdullahi Yusuf Ahmed

Secure Mogadishu from factional fighting and reconcile clan divisions. Install Yusuf's elected transitional government, currently in exile in Kenya

LIBERIA
Leader: Gyude Bryant
Disarm rebels after 2003 ceasefire. Prosecute exiled leader Charles Taylor, currently in Nigeria

KENYA
Leader: Mwai Kibaki

Stamp out corruption that drains billions amid massive poverty

DEMOCRATIC REPUBLIC OF CONGO
Leader: Joseph Kabila

Power-sharing Government, including former civil war rebels, must hold multiparty elections after 2003 ceasefire

ANGOLA
Leader: Jose Eduardo dos Santos

Protect human rights in separatist province. Return squandered oil money

ZIMBABWE
Leader: Robert Mugabe

Allow free elections and end human rights abuses against opposition to Government

UGANDA
Leader: Yoweri Museveni

Stop Museveni becoming President for life. End government corruption and crush Lord's Resistance Army rebels in the north

Conditions for the receipt of aid [10]

ACTIVITY 1: COMMENTARY

What criteria do we need to clarify our decision-making about the issue of world poverty?

There are some obvious ones that you probably came up with.

- Cost;

- Public opinion.

COST

This subject is one in which the **criterion of cost** is an obvious one. Perhaps it's the most obvious in that centrally the issue is about cost. How much would each option on the continuum cost? Even the option of military intervention comes with a (large) cost. Could we afford to enforce payment by military intervention? Similarly, of course, could we afford to cancel the debt?

Cost could prevent the choosing of certain options even if they could be justified by other criteria. In this way, it could be the most important criterion. In other words, if we can't afford to cancel all the debt, then that's pretty well the end of some of the options. Not all, of course, because we could still go for options (4) to (6).

The information on levels of aid could be used profitably here. The thrust of the information from the Oxfam report is that cancelling debts and giving more aid are both easily manageable. One response you could make is that, given that Oxfam is in the business of trying to reduce world poverty, you would expect it to argue in this way. (This is taking us back to the credibility focus you had in Unit 1 of the AS examination.) But this would not be a very useful response. We have no good reason to suppose that Oxfam, despite its (possible) vested interest in poverty-reduction, would invent evidence.

Just because a country gets less in aid than it pays out in debt repayment does not mean that this is a sufficient reason to cancel the debt. We would need to look at the background of such a situation to consider the reasons or this situation. However, one could bring this specific point about cost into our decision-making in order to argue that cancelling the debt could make the giving of aid more useful (options (7) to (10)). It could also lead us in the direction of options (4) and (5), in that both of these would reduce the imbalance between debt-repayment and aid.

The evidence on giving and receiving aid shows us a number of interesting points. The figures for donor nations are given in two ways: overall amount and amount as percentage of GDP. The figures for recipient nations are also given in two ways: overall amount and amount per head of population.

The overall figures show that the US is top of the donor nations (by far) and the Congo is top of the recipient nations (by far). However, the other figures show that, as a percentage of GDP, Saudi Arabia is top of the donor nations (by a noticeable amount) and, looking at amount of aid per head, French Polynesia is top of the recipient nations. Looking at the second lot of figures, the US comes out 26th as a donor nation and the Congo comes out 13th as a recipient nation.

,The list of donor nations by percentage of GDP could be used to show that rich countries could easily cover the cost of debt-relief and giving of further aid (thereby supporting (9) and (10)). The argument would be that small increases in GDP (as Oxfam argued) could make a big difference.

The list of recipient nations by head of population shows that money spent on aid might not meet the greatest need. For example, the two top recipient countries are both French overseas territories and are the recipients of much of France's overseas aid programme. Would we think that people in the West Bank and Gaza are in greater need than people in the Congo?

The evidence from Oxfam about global consumers spending $33 billion each year on cosmetics and perfume needs your Critical Thinking skills applied to it. Is it relevant? At one level, the figures might present a shocking imbalance between poverty and frivolous expenditure. At another level, they cannot be compared. The expenditure on cosmetic and perfume comes from individuals; expenditure needed to meet poverty-reduction targets is meant to come from governments. We'll have a further look at the significance of this evidence when we look at ethics.

PUBLIC OPINION

You will find that the **criterion of public opinion** will be relevant to virtually all of the decision-making that you'll be asked to do in Unit 3. Indeed, it could well be that it will be relevant to all of it. This is because we approach decision-making in the social, political, and economic spheres with an eye on what will be acceptable. For example, in various surveys of public opinion, we find that something like 50–60 per cent of the population is against the use of animals in experiments. If we were to look at a range of choices on this topic (which you could do), then any choices that include the use of animal experiments, however limited, would have to take into account the opposition of the public.

Public opinion on the subject of making poverty history might be seen as pretty favourable to the idea but, as always, we need to consider the evidence. We will now look at some that is relevant to this issue.

The following survey[11] was carried out during a time when there was a lot of public interest in the issue of poverty in developing countries. The results of the survey should therefore be significant in giving us an idea of what the public thought about the campaign to 'make poverty history'.

1   There is a lot of talk at the moment about the problem of poverty in Africa. How much do you personally feel you know about Africa and its problems?

A great deal	7
A certain amount	51
Not very much	37
Nothing at all	4
Don't know	2

2   Which THREE of the following factors do you think have contributed most to Africa's problems? [Tick up to three]

HIV/AIDS	53
Corrupt and incompetent African governments	79
Earlier neglect of sub-Saharan Africa by colonial governments	10
Exploitation of Africa by multinational companies and foreign investors	27
Overpopulation	25
Civil wars in Africa and fighting amongst African states	51
The trade and investment policies imposed by bodies such as the World Bank and the European Union	17
Lack of natural resources and a hostile climate	14
Don't know	4

3 Thinking mainly of Africa, but also of other impoverished parts of the world. Is it, in your view, possible to 'make poverty history'?

Yes, it is possible to make poverty history	39
No, it is not possible and the phrase is really just a slogan	49
Don't know	4

4 Thinking specifically of Africa, which of these statements do you think comes nearest to the truth?

Africans have it within their power to solve their own problems	30
Africans can solve their problems but only if they receive large-scale financial and other forms of assistance from rich countries	52
Africa's problems are insoluble – they cannot be solved	9
Don't know	9

5 Still thinking specifically of Africa, which of these statements do you think comes nearest to the truth?

It is up to Africans to solve Africa's problems	17
It is up to rich countries to solve Africa's problems	2
It is up to a partnership between Africans and rich countries to solve Africa's problems	70
Africa's problems cannot be solve by anybody	5
Don't know	6

6 Do you believe that Africans and African governments are by and large doing enough to help themselves?

Yes, they are	4
No, they are not	80
Don't know	15

7 On balance, which kinds of organisation do you think are better placed to help solve Africa's problems?

The governments of richer countries	10
International aid agencies and other non-governmental organisations such as War on Want and Oxfam	15
Both of these	53
Neither of these	13
Don't know	9

8 How confident are you that, if governments and people in richer countries donate more money to Africa, the money will be spent wisely rather than either being wasted or finding its way into the pockets of criminal and corrupt governments?

Very confident	1
Fairly confident	10
Not very confident	41
Not at all confident	42
Don't know	7

9 In response to the various appeals being made at the moment, do you expect to give more than you currently do to the charities in Africa?

Yes, I expect to give more money	10
No, I don't	51
I am not sure whether I will or not	34
Don't know	5

10 Suppose you decided, for whatever reason to give more money to charity during the next few weeks, which kinds of organisation would you be most likely to give to?

Domestic charities, such as Barnados and Help the Aged	42
Worldwide disaster relief charities, such as the Red Cross / Red Crescent	19
Charities heavily involved in Africa, such as Oxfam and War on Want	15
Don't know	25

11 It is suggested that the British government could assist African countries by cancelling all or most of the very large amounts of debt owed by African governments.

Do you personally think all or most of these debts should, or should not, be cancelled?

Yes, they should be	53
No, they should not be	28
Don't know	19

12 If the debts of African governments were cancelled, do you think reducing in that way their burden of debt and debt interest would, or would not, make a significant contribution towards solving Africa's problems?

Yes, it would make a significant contribution	47
No, it would not	38
Don't know	15

13 It is also suggested that, by protecting their domestic agriculture and subsiding agricultural imports, rich countries, including Britain and others in the European Union, are impoverishing farmers in Africa and making it difficult for them to compete on world markets.

Do you think that, in order to assist poorer countries, European agricultural subsidies should be abolished, even if that meant that British farmers would lose out?

Yes, I do	30
No, I do not	44
Don't know	25

What are we to make of this evidence in relation to public opinion as a criterion in making a decision from the positions on our continuum?

Is public opinion in favour of any of the options on our continuum?

Options that approve of dealing leniently with the problem of debt get little support from the responses to question 8. However, question 11 and, though a little less so, question 12 give support to these options. Question 3's responses, on the other hand, give no support to the idea that by cancelling debt, we can make poverty history. This is unlike the responses to question 4 which seem to indicate that people believe that we can solve the problem by at least, in part, providing financial support.

Question 8 points us, as we saw above, away from simply cancelling debt and more towards the seeing of problems in the giving of financial assistance without any guarantees as to how it is used. This could be used as support for either option (7) or (8) or, indeed, move us in the direction of enforcement of the debt.

Of course, public opinion can be ignored. There might be all sorts of reasons why, in this example, we could ignore it. Perhaps the public is misinformed. Perhaps, despite Bob Geldof's attempts to show the subject as simple, it's actually not simple and we don't think that the public understands it well enough. After all, when interest rates are set by the Bank of England each month, the team that meets to set the rate doesn't presumably worry about public opinion on the subject. It's a complex area which needs expert judgement.

We'll make reference to more of this survey material below.

We have so far looked at cost and public opinion as criteria that are relevant in helping us make a decision about options on our continuum. Both of these criteria are likely to be relevant to any issue that you are asked to deal with. But there will also be some *criteria that are specific to the particular issue* that you're looking at. We'll now turn our attention to these.

You might have come up with these specific criteria.

- The nature of the regime

- The extent of the problem of debt in each country

- The extent of need in each country

- The cause of the debt

- The way in which any aid has been used in the past

The nature of the regime is a very important criterion that is often overlooked in the slogan-chanting responses to the problem of debt. Do we treat all countries with debt the same?

The example of Robert Mugabe of Zimbabwe is a useful one. He is well-known for his suppression of dissent in his country, and also for presiding over the rapid decline of the Zimbabwean economy, turning a once-prosperous country into one with huge problems of malnourishment. His government has destroyed the temporary shelters that many city-living people had built, forcing them into a life of extreme poverty. Would this be relevant to whether or not any debts owed by the country should be paid?

You were given some evidence on the issue of human rights in various countries. Having looked at this, should we concentrate financial help in the countries on the second list rather than the first? This application of the criterion would certainly be relevant to option (6), but could also be used with option (8). Does this evidence make the criterion especially relevant?

The evidence showing the top ten recipients of aid and their human rights record could also be relevant here. There is no obvious correlation between giving aid and the achievement of a fair or good human rights record. (Perhaps there is no reason why there should be?) The evidence could also be relevant to another criterion.

A different (although probably related) issue that might be relevant here is the extent of corruption in different countries. Should we use this evidence to argue that the nature of the regime is significant in deciding what to do about debt-relief? At the top of the list of most corrupt countries is Bangladesh. In 2002, the Danish Government withdrew $45m of aid from the Bangladeshi shipping sector because of alleged corruption involving the shipping minister of that country. The Danish Government used the justification that they had an obligation to ensure that their money was properly spent in Bangladesh.

This evidence on corruption is relevant, therefore, to choices (6) to (8) in particular.

The survey on public attitudes to the 'make poverty history' campaign can provide us with further useful evidence here. Question 2 shows that many people see the nature of the regime as a problem. For example, 79 per cent of the respondents saw 'corrupt and incompetent African governments' as one of the factors that 'have contributed most to Africa's problems'.

The survey evidence gives us some support for the idea that help should not be given indiscriminately. Question 8 raises the issue of corruption and shows us that 83 per cent are either 'not very confident' or 'not at all confident' that money given won't end up in 'the pockets of criminals and corrupt governments.'

The map showing 'what the States should do in return for aid' is useful in linking the criterion of the nature of the regime with option (6) on the continuum. It helps us to see why the conditions could be important, by specifying how they could produce desired outcomes. You could also use this evidence to support option (8).

The extent of the problem of debt is a criterion that could be useful.

For example, do you need to know how much debt is owed by each country? How much debt as a proportion of the country's income? How much debt has already been paid?

The World Bank divides the countries of the world into four categories in terms of debt:

- severely indebted
- moderately indebted
- less indebted
- not classified by indebtedness

The UK falls (not surprisingly) into the last category along with a long list of West European and other countries. Countries in the first category include some expected ones – Angola, Burundi, Democratic Republic of Congo, Ethiopia, Nigeria, and Sudan are examples – and some possibly less expected ones – Argentina, Brazil, Estonia, Syria, and Turkey.

The category of 'moderately indebted' also, however, includes some countries that we might have expected to find in the first category: Benin, Burkina Faso, Ghana, Malawi, and Senegal are examples.

The 'less indebted' group includes Bangladesh, Botswana, Madagascar, Swaziland, and Uganda.

If we take the extent of debt to be an important criterion, then we would have to look at our continuum of choice using this criterion to help us make decisions.

Option (6) certainly fits with using this criterion. It could be that one could look at options in the range (2) to (4) for those countries that are less heavily indebted than others. It could be that (5) could be supported for those who are more indebted. Whether or not one could use this to support those from (7) to (10) is more problematic.

The extent of need in each country is another criterion.

At one level, just because a country is indebted does not mean that other countries should relieve it of that debt. But if a country has very high levels of poverty, it might be that need is an important criterion in the decision as to how to respond. This criterion of need is indeed used by those campaigning to 'make poverty history'. The Live 8 campaign stated that they will not 'tolerate the further pain of the poor'. In other words, poverty is seen as a sufficient justification for action.

The evidence on GDP amongst the poorest countries of the world (if GDP is the measure of poverty) shows that on this list there are, not surprisingly, countries that we have met in the other evidence that we have looked at. However, though Burundi is one that hasn't appeared before, we find familiar evidence. An ethnic war between the Tutsi minority and the Hutu majority has led to more than 200,000 deaths and created 450,000 refugees who fled to neighbouring Tanzania. A further 140,000 others were displaced within the country. High need is combined with huge political and social problems.

You might want to see the issue in terms of redistribution from high GDP nations to those with low GDPs. This is an issue we will return to when we look at ethics.

You were given two tables on life expectancy in different countries, showing the highest and lowest countries. The evidence on the latter again shows countries that we have been considering. Do those countries with a low life expectancy therefore demonstrate need? At what point does an increase in life expectancy reduce the level of need? For example, should more aid be given to Swaziland than, say, Ghana?

You will remember that we looked earlier at the figures for donor and recipient nations. The figures for amount of aid received by head of population showed that need was not necessarily the criterion used in deciding which countries should get what. If you look at that list, you might want to make the point that need is a much more effective criterion than others in making decisions about distribution. If donor countries are going to give anything, you could argue, they might as well give it in a way that maximises its purpose. However, that could be too naïve. After all, it does not take into account the value of a $ in each country. It could be that Burundi's $32 per head can purchase as much as (if not more than), say, Jordan's $301 per head.

The cause of the debt is another criterion you might have identified.

You could have used some of the evidence to both generate and support this criterion. For example, countries with a low life expectancy are very likely to find it difficult to develop economically. They will not have the labour force necessary to do this. Another source of evidence could have been that on corruption. Perhaps funding for important economic development was siphoned off by corrupt politicians and/or public officials (as in the example of Nigeria). This could then lead to the country having to borrow more or making it difficult to repay loans because of failed economic projects (or both).

Perhaps you would want to look at what the loans were used for. Some of the money might have gone to projects that didn't help the general population (such as the British aid for Swaziland). Perhaps you would want to look at the levels of military expenditure (if this was used to suppress opposition within a country).

Taking the criterion of the cause of the debt might have led you to consider historical factors such as the role of some countries (such as the UK) as rulers of many of the developing countries as colonies. In other words, the cause of these developing countries' debts could be linked to how their natural (and human) resources were used by the colonial powers. This is a huge area which would benefit from further study by you. It might lead you to justify either option (9)) or (10). The survey evidence could also be brought in here (although it's not that strong). Question 2 suggested that there is quite a range of answers that people gave as the cause of the problem. HIV/AIDS is suggested by 53 per cent; 'overpopulation' is given by 25 per cent; a minority look at historical (colonial) issues and current economic policies of richer countries.

The way in which any aid has been used in the past is a criterion that could be very relevant. Why should the international community not take account of the way in which a government has used aid in the past?

It could be useful to think of an analogy here with individuals who are in debt. If one individual is in debt because she was made redundant and, despite her best endeavours, can't get a job, we would presumably be sympathetic to her being helped. If another individual is in debt because she has spent her substantial lottery winnings on a whirl of flash holidays, cars, and handbags, then we would (presumably) be less sympathetic to helping her.

Is this analogy relevant? If it is, is the evidence on the King of Swaziland relevant here? Does this evidence enable us to make the use of aid an important criterion? It would be difficult to see how the use of aid could be seen as irrelevant to decision-making on this subject. One could certainly apply it to positions (6), (7), and (8) on the continuum. The conditions could be made clearer. For example, (8) could be developed such that the conditions specified that the cancellation of the debt was dependent on investments being made in the country's agriculture, industry, or education programme.

ACTIVITY 2

Having established some criteria that are relevant to helping decide what to do about the problem of debt-relief in developing countries, we are now in a position to consider what dilemmas we are faced with.

It would be helpful if you were able to express these in terms of the criteria that we have developed so far.

ACTIVITY 2: COMMENTARY

This should be a fairly straightforward exercise involving identifying conflicts between different criteria.

- Should cost be the criterion that determines how we should deal with debt in developing countries or should the nature of the regime?

- Should the nature of the regime be the criterion ... or should the need of the country for economic help?

- Should the extent of the debt in each country be the criterion ... or should the cause of the debt?

- Should the way in which aid has been used in the past be the criterion ... or should the extent of need in the country?

- Should public opinion in developed countries be the criterion ... or should cost be used instead?

And so on. The dilemmas that you are identifying emerge from a consideration of the criteria.

REFERENCES

(1) 'Where the money went: self-interest and stupidity', *The Times*, July 2 2005

(2) 'Why the West's billions may end up in the wrong hands, *The Times*, June 9 2005

(3) 'Aid to Africa', *The Times*, July 2 2005

(4) Based on 'Why the West's billions may end up in the wrong hands, *The Times*, June 9 2005 and 'Human Rights Report 2005', Amnesty International

(5) *The Economist Pocket World in Figures*, 2006 edition, Profile Books, 2005, p 63

(6) *The Economist Pocket World in Figures*, 2006 edition, Profile Books, 2005, p 28

(7) *The Economist Pocket World in Figures*, 2006 edition, Profile Books, 2005, pp 78 and 79

(8) 'Paying the Price' (summary), Oxfam, 2004, pp 3 and 4

(9) *The Economist Pocket World in Figures*, 2006 edition, Profile Books, 2005, pp 42 and 43

(10) *The Times*, July 6 2005

(11) YouGov/Daily Telegraph Survey on Africa, YouGov plc, 2005

5

INTRODUCING ETHICAL THEORIES

In the previous chapter, we considered the point that in coming to a conclusion as to what course of action was better than another, we need to consider both evidence and ethics.

Ethics is concerned with how we should live our lives. Should we be generous in giving to charities? Should we tell the truth? Should we keep our promises? By extension, then, it is also concerned with how societies should deal with how people should behave. Should abortion be allowed? Should we experiment on animals? Should we go to war? Individual and social/political/economic decisions will often conflict. Should I join the protests about the export of veal calves, though the Government has said that it will enforce the law through effective policing? Obviously, then, a human life without ethical problems is difficult to imagine.

Some ethical decisions have other implications. For example, the question 'should we have capital punishment?' has not only a large ethical component, but also an economic one. It could be argued (as some US websites argue) that keeping criminals in prison for life is too expensive, so we can justify executing them on economic grounds. The question 'should we look for intelligent life on other planets?' is one that has obvious scientific significance. But it also has ethical significance in that we might want to ask questions about how we can justify spending money on doing this rather than other things (health care being the obvious one).

The title of this chapter shows that we are going to introduce some ethical theories. For those who want much more detail, there are plenty of books available which will provide it. But, if we are going to do the job of applying ethical theories properly, we do need to be sufficiently clear as to their content. The idea that we can approach ethical theories by just seeing them as 'sound bites' is a dangerous one. 'Sound bites' by their very nature miss much of what surrounds them. They are what the true Critical Thinker reacts against. A sound bite approach to the solar system would be to say it's a pile of rock and gas, some of which is hot (and that's all you need to know to deal with questions such as 'has life developed on other planets?').

Of course, though at one level one can never know too much, there is also a danger that we can spend too long on the detail of the theories and forget why we're looking at them. We want to be able to use them to help us to decide what to do, to help us to resolve dilemmas. So this chapter will seek to tread the necessary line between the 'sound bite' and the over-detailed approach. The former is misleading; the latter is unnecessary.

What do we expect from an ethical theory? At the very least, it should offer some answer to an ethical problem that we have (even if it's an answer that we don't like).

A washing machine that doesn't give us washed clothes is of little (or no) value. Similarly, an ethical theory that doesn't offer us solutions to ethical problems is of little (or no) value.

Dirty sock → washing machine → clean sock

Ethical problem → ethical theory → ethical problem solved

If the ethical theory offers no solution to our problem, it is of limited value. ('Limited' rather than 'no', because it could still offer some insights, even though it doesn't go all the way to solving the problem.)

So, taking our dirty sock in our hand, we approach some washing machines on offer. How clean will our sock be at the end of the process? It's time to try them out.

We will consider three major ethical theories. There are others, but these three will be sufficient for you to answer questions in this Unit. We will outline the important content of the theories and apply them to real or hypothetical situations on the way. As we look at each one, we will apply it to problems that need solving, including looking again at some questions that have come up in previous chapters to see how it would help us to answer such questions.

The ethical theories are

• Utilitarianism

• Deontological ethics

• Libertarianism

UTILITARIANISM

You will have come across the word 'utility' before. It means 'usefulness'. The term 'utility room' shows this well, in that it refers to a room where useful appliances are kept (washing machine, dishwasher, tumble dryer, etc.). This meaning of 'usefulness' is significant. Those who look at ethics in terms of 'utility' are looking at what comes out of their ethical theory. They are interested in results (like we're interested in dry clothes coming out of a tumble dryer).

In the light of this, it is understandable why Utilitarianism is sometimes called a 'consequentialist' theory. This is because it is centrally concerned with the consequences of actions. What comes out of the process of applying a utilitarian position to a problem?

Ethical questions can be very small. For example, should I drop my empty crisp packet into a wastepaper bin? The utilitarian would be interested in that question in terms of what consequences it had. We'll return to this example later. A big question would be whether we should have invaded Iraq in 2003. The utilitarian would again be interested in the consequences of this action. We'll come back to this one later too.

What is it about the consequences that the utilitarian is interested in?

KILLING AND CONSEQUENCES

We'll start with a big issue. Let's consider the example of someone killing somebody else. What consequences of this action is the utilitarian interested in? In one form of the theory, they are interested in how such an action affects people's welfare. (We'll look in more detail below at what we mean by this.) In other words, we need to know more about the circumstances of the action in order to judge whether it was a good or bad one. Questions like 'Who was killed?' and 'Why were they killed?' become relevant.

You can see that a general position of 'all killing is wrong' is not one which fits with looking at the consequences of actions. A utilitarian can distinguish between actions in which somebody is killed as sometimes justifiable and sometimes not. To see how this might work, consider these different situations.

- Rudolf Höss, the first Commandant of Auschwitz, was hanged in 1947 as a punishment for his involvement in mass murder.

- Freddy Bywaters was hanged in January 1923 for the murder of his lover's husband.

- Derek Bentley was hanged in 1953 for being involved in an incident in which a policeman was shot, even though he didn't do the shooting.

In each of these cases, a legal process was used which led to the killing of someone. Is each of them to be seen in the same way? Were they all right (or wrong)? The utilitarian would need to look at the consequences of each of them.

If we are looking at the consequences of each in terms of the effect on 'welfare', how might this work? Perhaps the execution of Höss could be justified in terms of increasing the welfare of all those who suffered under him (but survived) and all those who had relatives who died as a result of his actions (directly or indirectly). We could also bring into the calculation all those who saw Nazism as so abhorrent that the death of such a prominent member of that movement was something that increased their welfare. Of course, we would have to set the welfare of the family and friends of Höss against all this. And the welfare of those who supported the Nazi cause. As a result, a calculation could be made to see if welfare had been increased by the execution of Höss. (I would think it was, but you might have done the calculation differently.)

The story of Freddy Bywaters is given in my 'Critical Thinking for AS Level' (pages 25–26). He killed only one man (unlike Höss). He had a mother, two sisters and a brother. His victim had a brother and two sisters. Neither man had children. Freddy's lover (the victim's wife) was hanged at the same time as him, having been convicted of conspiracy to murder. So can the execution of this twenty year-old be justified in terms of welfare or not? This is much more difficult than the case of Höss.

The case of Derek Bentley is one which caused huge controversy. He was only nineteen when he was hanged. He suffered significant learning difficulties, and was under arrest for an attempted robbery when his friend (whom the police had cornered but not yet caught) shot and killed a policeman. His friend was too young to be executed, but Bentley was hanged despite a huge public outcry. In 1998 he was given a full pardon.

The interesting thing from a utilitarian position is that this execution has been seen as helping the campaign which led to the abolition of the death penalty in this country (the last execution was in 1965). In an odd way then we could look back and say that, at one level, the welfare of many was subsequently improved by Bentley's execution (primarily abolitionists and convicted criminals and their families). Those who support the death penalty will have had their welfare reduced (as well as possibly some of those who have lost family members as a result of violent crime). In January 2006, only 49 per cent of the UK population supported the death penalty. We could look at that figure as showing us that there is a higher level of welfare for the UK population because we do not have the death penalty.

HAPPINESS, WELL-BEING, PLEASURE, AND OTHER GOOD THINGS

After considering these examples, it is time to take stock of where we are. The first big name associated with Utilitarianism is Jeremy Bentham (1748-1832). For him, there was something straightforward about what the utilitarian is looking for when we talk about 'welfare'. This is a quality of well-being that people feel. Think how you feel at the moment. Do you feel more or less happy than you did ten minutes ago? If reading this book is reducing your happiness at the moment, put it down, go and do something that will make you happy (of course, taking into account how this will affect others' happiness), and I'll see you later. (By the way, don't go off and read a Critical Thinking book by a different author: that'll make you only more miserable. I guarantee it.)

(Welcome back.) The classic utilitarian position as developed by Bentham looks at actions and judges them against a measure of happiness. You will remember the question of whether or not I should put my empty crisp packet in a wastepaper bin. Let's say I do put it in the bin. How does this fit with Bentham's equation for happiness? Perhaps it makes me feel happy to see the packet put in the right place, not left around as litter. Perhaps it makes others happy not seeing litter around. It's difficult to see how it can have reduced happiness, so it's probably an action which was right to do.

This Benthamite principle of justifying actions in terms of their effect on happiness is well-known as applying the rule of looking to maximise 'the greatest happiness of the greatest number'. This looks to be a simple yardstick to use. It has a familiar appeal to public opinion about it. Should we bring back the death penalty? No, because most people don't want it.

So far, then, we have been looking for a principle that we can use in deciding what course of action can be justified better than another one. The principle of utility involves calculating the effect on people's welfare. We have described this as well-being or happiness. More specifically, we should see it as 'felt' well-being or happiness. In other words, it's not just me reporting that you are happier, it's that you actually feel happier.

John Stuart Mill (who we met earlier when looking at the definition of freedom) thought that this way of looking at happiness as the way of calculating the justification of actions was too simple. It ignored the way in which different people experience happiness in different ways. Thus Mill argued that there are different levels of happiness. He is often quoted as saying that it is better to be a dissatisfied Socrates than a satisfied fool. Thus there are higher and lower pleasures. Listening to Mozart might be seen as a higher pleasure; watching Ipswich beat Norwich at football might be seen as a lower one. (Though I'm not so sure about the last one.)

We won't spend much time on this point, but we'll note its significance. This is that to work out the consequences of an action, policy, or decision might well be far more complicated than it seemed. There is, for example, the additional problem of how keenly a person feels about something. In this way, listening to Mozart might well give someone pleasure, but the joy of watching a football match could well be felt much more keenly. This point could also take us back to the problem of justifying capital punishment in particular cases. It could be that the knowledge that Höss had been executed was experienced as very high well-being by those who'd suffered at his hands. As a result, should this experience be counted as more important than how others experienced it?

A further way of looking at the utilitarian position is to look not at welfare, well-being, happiness or pleasure, but to look at preferences. A decision can be justified if it satisfies people's preferences. If it satisfies more people's preferences than a different decision, then we're OK. This gets round the higher/lower pleasures problem. We might have difficulties accepting some people's preferences, but at least we avoid having to make judgements about them.

You will probably already have thought that, at a very important level, all this talk of maximising preferences (or whatever) fits with the way in which much decision-making is done. International organisations such as the United Nations use a democratic voting system; small clubs do the same. To say that we shouldn't make decisions (political, social, economic, organisational, group, and even individual ones) according to people's preferences would be seen as, at least, odd. We would expect an explanation of why we shouldn't.

An example might illuminate this. When I worked in a prison, there was a nod in the direction of listening to what some of the young offenders had to say about things that affected them. ('Why can't we be allowed a hairdryer on the unit?' was an example.) However, when decisions were taken, they very often didn't reflect what the young men wanted. As a Principal Officer pointed out, 'this isn't a democracy'. In other words, the special features of a prison ensure that people's preferences do not necessarily have to be taken into account. (So no hairdryer.)

Let's look again at the continuum of choice we created for the question '*What should we do about violent computer games?'*

(A) Encourage people to play violent computer games in the hope of reducing the chances of them being violent themselves.

(B) Do nothing about the problem of violent computer games.

(C) Commission further research in order to demonstrate any effects of violent computer games.

(D) Encourage parents to exercise control over their children by monitoring what games they play.

(E) Restrict the sales of the most violent computer games only to those aged 18 or over.

(F) Restrict the sales of all computer games in which violence is portrayed only to those aged 18 or over.

(G) Ban all computer games for which there is any evidence linking them with violent behaviour.

(H) Ban all computer games in which the violence is more than 'mild'.

(I) Ban all computer games in which there is any violence.

How might a **utilitarian perspective** help us to decide which to go for? There would be lots of things to have to take into account. For example, we can't ignore the fact that behaving violently might produce lots of happiness for some people, be their preference, and so on. But we'll look at our options in as simple way as possible.

(G), (H), and (I) could have a problem in relation to the preferences (happiness, pleasure, well-being) of those who play these games. Alternatively, we could look at the preferences (etc.) of those who want these games banned. If there was evidence showing that these games did increase the likelihood that players used violence, then we would also have to look at the well-being (etc.) of those who would be the victims. But what about the welfare of games-producers, distributors, sellers, reviewers, etc?

(E) and (F) restrict the preferences (etc.) of those under 18. We might not think this is a problem. After all, we don't give the vote to those under 18. But if lots of young people found their welfare much reduced by these decisions, then we have to be able to answer the charge that welfare has been reduced. How would you do that?

(A) has a welfare-maximising look about it. We could justify this proposal in terms of the consequences. If playing the games made people less violent, then welfare is increased on a big scale. (Unless you're a police or prison officer, in that you might be made redundant.) There is, of course, the problem that we might have got it wrong. Encouraging people to play the games could make them more violent.

(B) can be supported by the utilitarian if doing nothing maximises welfare. This would work if any adverse effects of people playing violent computer games were more than compensated for by the overall level of welfare resulting from doing nothing. For example, we would need to add in the welfare of players (and that of the games-producers, etc.), and the fact that presumably most people aren't too worried about the whole issue.

(C) looks to a future situation in which we can maximise welfare only by knowing more about the problem. It can be defended in a utilitarian way by arguing that, once we have established whether or not there are any effects (good or bad), then we can act to maximise welfare.

(D) works to maximise welfare by coming up with a solution which could have good effects on overall welfare. The welfare of the controlled children might well be reduced but, if there are bad effects of these games, then this reduction in welfare could be defended.

We have seen then that a utilitarian position can illuminate decision-making. We have identified some problems on the way, but we can now turn our attention to looking more explicitly at problems with this position. Can the utilitarian washing machine produce an ethically-clean sock?

How can we apply utilitarianism to actual decision-making?

We're going to look at how workable this ethical theory is. In that we're looking at an ethical theory earning its keep in terms of how much it helps us make decisions, this is very important. Some questions will throw light on what we need to consider.

- How can we rate different types of pleasure?
- How do we rate different levels of experiencing pleasure?
- How can we establish what people's preferences are?
- What if someone's (or some group's) preferences change?
- Whose preferences should we take into account?
- How do we know if or when we have maximised welfare?

Now let's examine these questions individually.

How can we rate different types of pleasure?
How do we rate different levels of experiencing pleasure?

The first and second questions both share the same problem of how we do the necessary calculation of expected pleasure, etc. Even if we have to make very small-scale choices, the calculation of expected welfare is not necessarily easy. Let us suppose you're faced with a choice between two holiday destinations. If you'd like to go to either of them, how do you do the happiness-calculation? You would look at things like facilities, weather, cost, and journey-times. But, even then, we probably can't give exact figures for our calculation. (How do you rate two rather than two and a half hours on the plane?) What about all the less predictable factors? What about seeing poverty or cruelty to animals at your destination? How do you add those in?

The response is, of course, that you might be satisfied with an overall judgement, rather than, say, being able to produce a result which can be expressed in exact terms (a welfare calculation of, say, +14 contrasted with one of –6). You probably will be, because that fits with how you make decisions anyway. And, in a similar way, we can't expect governments to do the happiness-calculation in a very, very detailed form. Perhaps all that we can expect is that they're in the right direction.

How can we establish what people's preferences are?

Trying to find out what people's preferences are is a very big and complex area. We haven't got time to go into it, because you're looking at important variables such as honesty, needs/wants, and maturity.

There are, however, many times when we wouldn't have to ask for people's preferences. There are some preferences that, by and large, we can take for granted. For example, should we have a policy to require that all girls are called Daisy? I don't even have to go and ask people to know where their preferences lie. We can answer questions like this on the basis of our own judgement, which we can safely generalise to most (all?) others. At Oxford station (and probably many others), you see some barriers which are topped by very spiked metal constructions. The intention of these sharply-spiked barriers is obviously to deter us from climbing over them. Those who installed them didn't have to make much of a judgement as to how unappealing these would be to our welfare. They were correct in assessing them as something that most of us would rather not end up climbing over.

What if someone's (or some group's) preferences change?

The example of the invasion of Iraq is relevant to the fourth question. When the UK Government made the decision to be part of the invasion force, the majority of the UK population supported the decision. This support, however, declined until only a minority supported it. So was the decision right or wrong using this particular application of the principle? Could it be both right and wrong? (Of course, there are lots more applications of the principle needed to get the full account of preferences in this example.)

Whose preferences should we take into account?

The fifth question is an important one. Should everyone's preferences be taken into account? Anyway, what do we mean by 'everyone'? Does it include children? Does it include animals? Does it include future generations of people? Does it include everyone in the world? Some of these questions will apply with greater force to some decisions than to others. For example, whether we should take steps to reduce global warming (if it is happening) is a decision that involves a huge number of preferences. For example, am I required to care about the fact that much of Norfolk (and London) might disappear under water by 3000? If so, do I also have to worry about what might happen in the year 3050? When does it stop?

The question 'should we use experiments on animals to research cystic fibrosis?' is one where we need to consider whose preferences are to be taken into account. Is it just those families which have a child with the condition (or whose adults carry the gene responsible for the condition)? What about those who are opposed to animal experimentation? What about research staff who work in this area? And, of course, what about the welfare/well-being/happiness/preferences of animals that will be used?

How do we know if or when we have maximised welfare?

The final question is a very difficult one. It's not as if, having done the happiness calculation, we hear a bell ring showing we've maximised it. We never really know when we've done it, especially when we're looking at decision-making on a big scale. But, apart from the difficulties identified when looking at the earlier questions in this section, there's a separate but very important point relevant to this question. Quite simply, we don't know what would have happened if we hadn't implemented this decision.

Let's say we ban all computer games in which there is any violence (option (I)). In calculating the effects of this, we can't know what doing nothing (option B) would have done in relation to people's preferences. We can't rerun the tape to see. In this way, maximising welfare becomes difficult to judge.

If we think again about the 2003 invasion of Iraq, then this problem is very much highlighted. At what point can we say that it was right or wrong in terms of the impact on welfare? Even if the welfare of the Iraqi people might be seen as lower than it was before the invasion, might there not come a point at which it is higher (thanks to the invasion)?

Does utilitarianism allow for extreme positions to be adopted?

Though we might find the idea somewhat unpleasant, historical evidence shows that public executions were very popular. People often queued for the best vantage points, especially when the victim's crime was well-known. In that, given the opportunity, we might be the same, could we support a proposal to have public executions back in our towns and cities?

If we are setting out to maximise preferences, then we could imagine a situation in which we could support not only reintroducing capital punishment but also making them public. There are countries today (Iran is a notable example) which have public executions. This situation would be one in which enough people expressed a preference for such spectacles. In this way, we could defend them ethically.

However, we do need take into account the welfare of those who would be revolted by such a spectacle. In addition, in this calculation, we must include our own preferences. If we could not tolerate being publicly executed ourselves, then why should we tolerate it for others?

Does utilitarianism help us to know how to distribute scarce resources?

Many decisions involve the question of how we should distribute welfare amongst the population. For example, there have been recent campaigns concerned with demands that all people who need them should receive specific drugs through the National Health Service (NHS). This is a real issue and it is not necessarily easily resolved. Just to say 'give them all the drugs' is likely to ignore the complexities of the problem. In one recent case, protests that people with brain tumours should all receive a specific course of drug treatment was countered by an NHS decision-maker with the point that, if that were to happen, then there would be a knock-on effect elsewhere to cover the cost (say, fewer hip replacements or scanning machines).

Let's look at this with an imaginary example. In this example, a country's population can be broken down into five groups, based on their existing levels of welfare.

10% of the population has very low levels of welfare (through poverty, for example).
15% of the population has low levels of welfare.
50% of the population has moderate levels of welfare.
15% of the population has high levels of welfare.
10% of the population has very high levels of welfare (through considerable affluence, for example).

In the example, there are 1,000,000 people in the country.

These are therefore distributed as follows.

100,000 people with very low levels of welfare
150,000 people with low levels of welfare
500,000 people with moderate levels of welfare
150,000 people with high levels of welfare
100,000 people with very high levels of welfare

A new drug is available that could cure a life-threatening disease. But the health service can't afford to give this drug to all who need it. In this country, there are 200 people with the life-threatening disease, distributed evenly amongst the welfare groups (the disease is no respecter of felt welfare). The health service has enough funding to give the drug to only 100 people. Who should these be?

If it gave the drug to 20 from each category, then what happens? It means that the level of welfare has stayed the same.

Perhaps the policy could be adopted of giving the drug to the 40 people in the very low welfare group and the 40 in the low welfare group, with the remaining 20 coming from the moderate welfare group. This could be a policy of 'positive discrimination', concentrating resources where there is least welfare. But what would be the outcome of this policy? Quite simply, the level of overall welfare would decline. We would lose people from the high and very high welfare groups, with insufficient compensatory gain.

What then happens if we give the drug to the 40 in the high welfare group and to the 40 in the very high welfare group, with the remaining 20 who get the group from those with moderate welfare? Given that people in the low and very low welfare groups now die, our overall level of welfare has increased. As simple as that.

Of course, for a full calculation of consequences for welfare, we would need to look at the welfare of all those who would be affected by our decisions. For example, person P from the very high welfare group might have no family and friends and thus their death would be unmourned. Q, however, from the very low welfare group might be greatly mourned by his seven children. (Think of Scrooge and Bob Cratchett in Dickens' 'Christmas Carol')

At one level, then, the utilitarian position allows us to see that an uncritical nod in the direction of equality might not be an ethically defensible thing to do. In terms of decision-making, the position provides at the very least a practical framework for choosing between different options.

The previous discussion has hinted at how utilitarianism can provide rules for how we ought to act. It is perhaps not surprising therefore that there is a version of the theory called 'rule utilitarianism'. This is particularly relevant to the sort of decision-making that we are concerned with in this Unit. A rule utilitarian position is one which says that we should act in ways that, if everybody were to act like this, welfare would be maximised. For example, if everybody put their crisp packets in wastepaper bins rather than dropping them all over the place, overall welfare would be greater. Therefore each of us should put our crisp packet in a bin. This rule avoids us having to get caught up with individual exceptions, such as an eccentric person who collects empty crisp packets as a hobby (but only those that have not been put in a bin).

Doesn't utilitarianism merely encourage selfishness?

In that we have been looking at criteria such as pleasure, happiness, and preferences, it might be thought that utilitarianism is just a licence to maximise our own pleasures without a thought for anyone else.

There is a companion ethical theory called 'egoism'. ('Ego' is the Latin for 'I'.) This theory is concerned with the need for each person to act in ways that maximise their welfare. This does not mean that a person living their life according to this theory will act in ways that do not consider others. For example, you might *want* to act in ways that take other people's feelings or interest into account. You might *want* to devote yourself to the care of others.

We won't concern ourselves too much with egoism here because we are looking at how ethical theories can help us with decision-making on a scale beyond the individual. It can be noted, however, that egoism avoids some of the problems with utilitarianism. The obvious one is that we don't have to try to calculate preferences across the board: just your own is enough.

We now need to move from utility to duty. Will an ethical washing machine using duty as the detergent get our sock any cleaner?

DEONTOLOGICAL ETHICS

We have seen that utilitarianism focuses on the consequences of actions: an action is right if it maximises welfare. In this way, the utilitarian is concerned with what follows a decision rather than the decision itself. If we disagree with a particular decision, the utilitarian could say 'wait until you see what happens, and then you'll see that the decision was right.'

But we might want to respond that we don't think that the decision was right full stop. Whatever the consequences, the decision might be one that we find ethically unacceptable. For example, when we look back at our continuum of choice for violent computer games (page 68), we might find (A) ethically unacceptable, even if it did lead to people becoming less violent. We might want to say that there is something unacceptable about children playing violent games and that's enough to rule out (A).

This emphasis upon choices being right or wrong in themselves finds us in the system of ethics called 'deontological'. The term 'deontological' comes from two Greek words: *deon* meaning 'duty' and *logos* meaning 'science' (think of words such as psychology and sociology). The two components of the word are both important for an understanding of the significance of the term.

The name normally associated with duty ethics is Immanuel Kant (1724-1804). There are many aspects of Kant's account of ethics, and we shall concentrate only on how we can apply a deontological position to decision-making. The link between 'duty' and 'science' is, for Kant, a central point. The study of how we should behave and the laws of nature are, for him, linked. In other words, we can study both of these subjects as rational creatures. How we should behave is therefore a question that can be answered, if you like, scientifically.

Kant argued that if we look at all life (animal and plant), then every part of an organism has a purpose. In fish, fins are there to help them swim; in dogs, their considerable ability to analyse scents is useful for hunting. Animals, he argued, are controlled by instinct: the bee, for example, does not seek out pollen as a result of reflecting on what to do with his day. Humans, however, are more than instinct, since they have the capacity to reason. Thus, according to Kant, if the pursuit of happiness was enough for us, we wouldn't need reason. Animals can seek to maximise their welfare through instinct. We must do something other than this.

Kant argued that all rational human beings would (have to) agree on what is the general duty which can be applied to all situations. It is actually much stronger than 'can be applied': Kant saw the duty as being an absolute one, such that rational people would *have to* apply it. It's like saying 'should I use this 100 centimetre ruler as the one to mark out metres or should I use the 110 centimetre one?' The question has only one answer for a rational person.

ETHICAL DUTIES

So what is this ethical duty which we must accept?

Kant argued that we should act only in such a way that we could accept that this way of acting should apply to everyone.

It will be helpful to consider how this might work in practice. Consider why telling the truth is something that we should do. How would it fit with Kant's required ethical duty? If we look at what would happen if everyone lied, then we could not wish this to be required action. If everyone lied, communication would be impossible. So I cannot wish it to be a universal law that everyone lies. It becomes therefore a duty to tell the truth. Though this looks like an example of rule utilitarianism, it has an important difference. We are not justifying telling the truth in terms of welfare, but in terms of the impossibility of a rational person wanting the lack of truth-telling to be the norm. You could try the same exercise with keeping promises.

Kant's account could be seen as having the problem of not allowing exceptions. The absolute duty not to lie has a problem in that we can think of situations where telling a lie could be seen as an entirely acceptable thing to do.

HOW DO WE SEE ETHICAL DUTIES?

But has Kant come up with something that fits well with how we see the world? Though there will be some things that might have a value (keeping promises, telling the truth, being considerate to others, and so on) relative to the situation in which we find ourselves, are there some actions that we can never accept, regardless of the consequences? What about killing a child? In Martin Gilbert's book 'The Holocaust', he describes an event in which German soldiers attacked a hospital and threw babies out of an upper-storey window for their comrades below to catch on their bayonets. Why is it that your reaction to that information is, I expect, the same as mine? Are we both using an absolute moral judgement, such that we can never accept that this is justified? (However, try something similar with some time-travel involved. Let's suppose you've managed to arrive back in 1889, in the Austrian town of Braunau. You make your way to the house of a minor customs official and, with the door open, you head upstairs and see a sleeping baby. This is little Adolf Hitler. There is a pillow in the room. All you've got to do is to quietly smother the little baby. Then you can get back into your time machine and come back again. Do you do it?)

Ignoring the killing of baby Adolf, has Kant got things right on the killing of children? Indeed, Kant went further and argued that there is an absolute moral duty not to kill innocent people. (He had no problem with killing animals or justifying the execution of murderers.) Some recent evidence might suggest that there is a problem in how we perceive this moral duty.

In a study, volunteers were given two problems. In the first, a runaway train threatens to kill five people, but their deaths can be prevented by a bystander throwing a lever, causing one person on the train to die. In the second, the bystander can save the five by throwing someone in front of the train, thus killing this person. Though both cases involve killing one person to save five, most thought it correct to do so in the first but not the second case. Brain scans of the volunteers revealed that they used the logical part of the brain to solve the first problem, but the part of the brain that deals with emotions to solve the second.

So Kant is faced here with the problem that we don't always approach moral problems rationally. Our brains appear to be 'hard-wired' to prevent us being as thoroughly Kantian as we might like to be. However, the study also shows that we're not as utilitarian as we might seem to be. In both cases, the principle of utility would point us in the direction of pushing someone on the track to save the people in the train.

Various studies have looked at how people would approach decision-making in health care. They show an interesting combination of utilitarian and deontological approaches. In one study in Brazil[1], members of the public were asked to make choices as to who should get treatment between different types of patient. For example, if a seven year-old child and a sixty-five year-old man were both victims of a car accident, which of them should get a hospital bed? 72% said that the child should get the bed. The justifications included deontological reasons – 'The child must be protected' – and utilitarian ones – 'The life expectancy and potential of the child is greater'. When the two cases were a twenty-five year-old man and one who was sixty-five, 61% chose the older man. Justifications included the deontological 'He is older, therefore he is weaker'. However, some of the 36% who chose the younger man reasoned that 'The younger one has to be attended first because he can do useful work.'

What studies such as this one show is that making decisions can, in practice, involve more than one ethical theory. The way we make choices is not necessarily either utilitarian or deontological, but a combination of the two.

APPLYING THE ETHICS OF DUTY TO DECISION-MAKING

But let's see if we can start applying a deontological framework to decision-making. We will return to the continuum of choice as to what to do with violent computer games. We're now going to look at where absolute moral duties are going to take us with this problem. Gone is talk of maximising preferences for the different policies. We will need to judge them against the requirement of moral duties, such that we are concerned with the morality of the decision itself.

If we take it that we have an absolute moral duty not to kill innocent people, then we can consider that we have a similar duty to prevent violence against innocent people. It surely can't be right to almost kill an innocent person, but not to kill them. How would this apply to our continuum on violent computer games? If it could be shown that violent computer games did contribute to violence, then we are looking at a moral duty to ban them. If the case is yet to be proved, then we must justify decisions on the basis of having a moral duty to reduce the risk of harm to innocent people. Let's have this in front of us whilst we're doing this exercise.

(A)   Encourage people to play violent computer games in the hope of reducing the chances of them being violent themselves.

(B)   Do nothing about the problem of violent computer games.

(C)   Commission further research in order to demonstrate any effects of violent computer games.

(D)   Encourage parents to exercise control over their children by monitoring what games they play.

(E)   Restrict the sales of the most violent computer games only to those aged 18 or over.

(F)   Restrict the sales of all computer games in which violence is portrayed only to those aged 18 or over.

(G)   Ban all computer games for which there is any evidence linking them with violent behaviour.

(H)   Ban all computer games in which the violence is more than 'mild'.

(I)   Ban all computer games in which there is any violence.

We could take a precautionary position and defend all those from (E) to (I) on the basis that these could fit with our moral duty to prevent harm. (B) is a problem for our moral duty position if we are concerned with the possibility of harm. Indeed (B) can be justified deontologically only if it could be shown that our moral duty not to harm others is best served by doing nothing. (C) could be defended on the grounds that we should do this in order to be clearer as to how our moral duty to prevent harm fits with the problem. Of course, we could justify doing any of (E) to (I) and also (C) together on the same basis. This leaves (A) and (D). We could defend (A) but only if we have evidence that it would work to prevent harm. Without such evidence, we appear to be treating our moral duty in rather a weak way. (D) could be supported if it worked. We might need to remind parents of their moral duty to prevent harm for this to work. In consequence, 'encourage' looks too weak. 'Require' would fit better with a moral duty.

DIFFERENT RULES?

Some writers have referred to a set of rules that are absolute; others have seen the need to balance some rules against others. The way in which the rules are interpreted can also vary. For example, W D Ross argued that we have a duty to do as much good as possible. Other deontologists have responded by saying that this duty of 'beneficence' means no more than being required to do *something* for those who are in need. Some have argued that our duties are not as demanding as they appear. If we are not in breach of our duty, they would argue that we can do what we like in our own time. We can, of course, also go beyond duty. Those people who are awarded the Victoria Cross 'for valour', for action way beyond the call of duty in battle are good examples.

DUTIES, ENDS, AND MEANS

We have so far stressed that the deontological position requires us to focus on duty as the basis for our decision-making. However, things are rather more complicated than that. Kant stressed that the ability to act as an autonomous person was the central thing that we should ensure. In other words, the ability to determine the way in which we lead our life was something that could not be traded off against other things (such as maximising people's preferences). Kant tapped into a very old idea of not treating people as means to ends. To take autonomous people and simply use them as a means to an end (however good this end might be) cannot be justified.

JOHN RAWLS

Another name of note in the deontological position is that of John Rawls (1921-2002). His book *A Theory of Justice* was one of the most important books of the second half of the twentieth century. We have not got space to look at his theory, but we can note some things that you might find useful (hopefully avoiding the 'sound bite' approach).

The veil of ignorance

John Rawls developed the idea of considering what sort of society we would have if we had to choose behind what he called a **veil of ignorance**. This works by requiring us to make choices on questions like 'Should we tolerate poverty?' 'Should we discriminate on the grounds of age in relation to jobs?' 'Should we prevent some groups of people from having health care, such as expensive drugs?' But, behind the veil of ignorance, we make the choices without knowing anything about who we would be in our society. For all we know we could be poor, homeless, very sick, and so on. We could be male or female, young or old, attractive or unattractive. If we wouldn't be prepared to accept any position in the society that we're agreeing to behind the 'veil of ignorance', then we can't justify it for others. If I'm not prepared to be homeless, why should I accept that others could be?

This idea of the 'veil of ignorance' has been criticised for being something that it is impossible to apply. We can't imagine ourselves in a disembodied form, having no idea of our age, gender, ethnic group, and so on. But the idea still has value in focusing us on whether or not we can justify inequalities. It might well be that we could accept being less affluent than others, as long as our position was still tolerable.

The Difference Principle

This brings us to another of Rawls' ideas. This is known as the **Difference Principle**. By this he means that we can tolerate social and economic differences if they work to the benefit of the least advantaged. A good example could be the considerable wealth held by some people (Richard Branson, Alan Sugar, and so on). If it could be shown that the wealth of such people benefited not only them, but also the least advantaged people in our society, then we can tolerate their being so wealthy. An obvious example of such a benefit would be employment. People can get jobs in Virgin Record shops and in shops selling Amstrad products. Try out the Difference Principle on other examples of inequality (for example, the monarchy).

You are likely to find these two ideas of Rawls – the veil of ignorance and the Difference Principle – helpful in considering choices available to you on the continuum of choice.

Rawls was critical of the utilitarians because their position would not fit well with either the veil of ignorance or the Difference Principle. He goes as far as saying that behind the veil of ignorance, we wouldn't pick utilitarianism as a guide to what we should do. He points out that one of the problems with it is that it doesn't distinguish between different desires. For example, someone who wants to discriminate on the grounds of age ('you can't have that job any more because your hair is grey') might be allowed to exercise that preference in utilitarianism, but not with his position.

We'll have a look at how the Rawlsian position would help us in decision-making later.

LIBERTARIANISM

Rawls (and Kant) saw the notion of a right as a central feature in their ethics. Rawls argues that we shouldn't be neutral about taking into account people's preferences. If you enjoy seeing other people enjoy much less welfare than you do, then you are not *entitled* to this enjoyment. Your enjoyment is wrong because it goes against a principle that you would have agreed behind the veil of ignorance. Thus Rawls is not looking to maximise preferences whatever they are. He is stressing that the idea of a *right* comes before the idea of preferences.

However, there are rights and there are rights. The libertarian (as the word suggests) is concerned with liberty. Indeed, their concern for liberty is paramount. Just as the utilitarian is concerned with maximising preferences, and the deontologist is concerned with stressing duty, so the libertarian is concerned with preserving freedom. We sometimes see the term used in newspaper accounts referring to people (normally in the Conservative Party) who think that the State has gone too far. For example, some libertarians argue that the State should not get involved with restricting the use of presently illegal drugs or regulating sexual behaviour.

ROBERT NOZICK

Libertarians focus on the relationship between the individual and the State. In doing this, they start from the position of the rights of the individual. These come first and the State has to respect them. Though there are many libertarian writers, there is one who is the most significant of recent times. This is Robert Nozick (1938-2002). In some ways, his book *Anarchy, State, and Utopia* was a libertarian response to Rawls. Interestingly, Kant's emphasis on not treating people as means to ends finds a home with Nozick just as it had with Rawls. However, with Nozick, this idea justifies the almost over-riding rights of the individual.

In some ways, Nozick's theory is very simple. Imagine that you're one of the first people to arrive at a previously undiscovered island. Nobody else lives there. You have got acres of uncultivated land available. In order to live, you start cultivating the land, growing a range of fruit and vegetables. You work hour after hour in the hot sun in looking after your plants. The other people who came to this land with you are busy getting on with cultivating their plants in their own parts of the island. Everything is as it should be. Then, one day, another ship arrives at your island. The people from the ship come on to your island and, being hungry (and less disposed to work hard), they start to pick your fruit and vegetables. Despite your protests that this produce is yours, they gorge themselves day after day on what you have grown. You'd feel pretty aggrieved, wouldn't you?

Why do you feel aggrieved? Because your property has been stolen? That you've worked hard for months to create your fruit and vegetables? That the newcomers have no right to them? If so, welcome to Nozick's world.

Nozick starts from the position that people have a moral right of ownership to themselves. You own yourself; I own myself. (Straightaway you can see that there's going to be a collision with utilitarianism in which your interests can be sacrificed for the greater good.) Having arrived on my island, as a distinct moral person with rights attached to me, I then use myself to change the nature of the island. Remember that I'm not taking the land from anybody, but what I am doing is to mix my labour with the land to create a product. Not only is the product mine (the strawberries, potatoes, etc.), but so is the land that I've now cultivated. It is now in a form that will make it easier to grow more crops. So you need to say to this lot who've come to your island and are stealing your crops: 'Go and cultivate your own piece of land as I did with this. Then that land will belong to you, just as this belongs to me'. You might, of course, choose to give these people some of your produce to help them on their way. But, as Nozick would stress, you are not required to.

Now bring yourself off the island and back to the present-day UK. For Nozick, the context has changed but not the ethical theory. Each day, people go to work (mixing their labour with something to create a product or service). Each pay day, they are paid only part of what they earn. The rest goes in taxation. So each pay day, someone comes along and steals some of your strawberries and potatoes. For Nozick, this is completely unacceptable. It means that you no longer own yourself. Your moral right to your self has been taken away. Kant's requirement that people should not be treated as means rather than ends has been violated.

So where does this position take us? The Welfare State becomes a form of slavery, in that it is paid for by requiring people to pay for others. When university students protest loudly about having to pay fees, they are saying to the rest of us 'We are entitled to your money, whether or not you want to give it to us'.

There are various problems with Nozick's position. For one thing, it presents an oversimplified account of property rights. On our imaginary island, his theory seemed to work well. In a sophisticated modern economy, it is much more difficult to apply it. We are much more inter-connected than the people on the island. To get from A to B, for example, requires me to expect that all sorts of people have co-operated to ensure that I can.

There is also the problem of ownership. On my uninhabited island, I didn't have to worry about people already owning bits of it. But in our society, things have already been largely packaged up into people's existing property rights. The Queen has the largest private art collection in the world. All those Leonardos, Rembrandts, and Van Dykes are hers, not yours and mine. But did she mix her labour with anything to get them? What about property that was gained hundreds of years ago by unacceptable means (theft, murder, fraud)? How can we get that back?

You can see that Nozick's position will have a lot to say about decision-making which requires us to distribute resources from one group to another. We will meet it again in this connection.

ISSUES OF DISTRIBUTION OF RESOURCES

Many decision-making dilemmas are indeed to do with how we should distribute resources. We met one such dilemma when we looked at the problem of how to distribute a life-saving drug, and applied a utilitarian perspective to the problem. But there are other ways we can approach such problems.

Scarce resources can be distributed according to

*   need;

*   desert;

*   rights.

Need is a familiar criterion to use in deciding who should get what. It's one of the principles used in the distribution of welfare resources in this country.

*   Who should get help from the NHS?

*   Who should get financial help from the Welfare State?

These questions (and many more like them) could all be answered with the answer 'those who need it'. The sick and the poor would both come into the category of need.

How need is defined is a question that requires an answer. It could be defined in terms of income levels, housing conditions, medical condition, educational performance, and so on. It could be a combination of these.

Obviously Nozick would have none of this. The fact that you need help has no necessary ethical significance for me. I might choose to respond but your need is more your problem rather than mine. The utilitarian might be interested in responding to need, but it would depend on the outcome of doing so. Would it be the most effective way of maximising preferences? Deontologists such as Rawls would be very sympathetic to looking at need. People in considerable need will find it very difficult to be autonomous, and anyway what about the problem of justifying not responding to need from behind the veil of ignorance?

Desert is a criterion that looks at the problem very differently. It asks the question 'what people deserve to be helped?' It often comes up as an issue with welfare resources. Let's consider the same questions as before.

- Who should get help from the NHS?
- Who should get financial help from the Welfare State?

The answers now are not the same. Who deserves to get help from the NHS? Think of this question in relation to the smoking debate. The point has been made many times that those people who smoke do not deserve help when they are ill in the same way as those who don't. When George Best was given a liver transplant, there was a debate as to whether, as a result of his very heavy drinking, he deserved to have one.

Who should get financial help from the Welfare State? Those who have not wasted money that they'd got? Those who would spend the money wisely? Those who've lived law-abiding lives? People who've given up their job are not immediately entitled to help from the State. Why? Because it's seen that they don't deserve it.

Rights is a response that is different again. Instead of looking at who needs help or who deserves it, we now consider who has a right to help. This is very often a simple case of who's entitled to help because of a legal entitlement. If you pay pension contributions over a minimum number of years, then you're entitled to draw that pension when the time comes. Even if you're a multi-millionaire or you've led a life of unbridled debauchery, you're entitled to your pension because you've entered into a contract which says you are.

This issue has come up with a couple of winners of the National Lottery. Michael Carroll, sometimes referred to as the 'lotto lout' has been seen as someone who did not deserve to win the jackpot (being in prison at the time). But, of course, he had a right to his £9.7 million because he had a ticket whose numbers matched those that were drawn. The other case was that of a convicted rapist who won the jackpot. Talk of not allowing such people to keep their money raises huge questions. Who then should win the jackpot? Those who deserve to? Those who need to?

Of course, a system of welfare can use all of these criteria. Our Welfare State does indeed distribute resources on the basis of need, desert, and rights.

ACTIVITY 1

In previous chapters we have produced both a continuum of choice and criteria for the subject of debt-relief in developing countries.

The continuum of choice we have used is given below.

(1) If no payment made, and sanctions not effective, military intervention to be used to seize property as payment of debt.

(2) Enforce payment of the debt, with sanctions to be applied if payments not made.

(3) Enforce payment of the debt.

(4) Enforce payment of only part of the debt.

(5) Make payment of the debt easier by extending the repayment period.

(6) Treat different countries differently.

(7) Cancel the debt, with conditions for all countries.

(8) Cancel the debt, with conditions for some countries.

(9) Cancel the debt, and provide financial help.

(10) Cancel the debt, provide financial help, and provide other help, such as medical care, agricultural products, and so on.

The criteria that we have looked at were these.

• Cost

• Public opinion

• The nature of the regime

• The extent of the problem of debt in each country

• The extent of need in each country

• The cause of the debt

• The way in which any aid has been used in the past

There is clearly a range of options that we can choose.

(a) To focus yourself on seeing how ethical theories can help in making this choice, look first at the conflict between the nature of the regime and the extent of need. How would the three ethical theories we have looked at clarify our decision-making in this conflict?

(b) Now look at the two criteria of cost and public opinion. How would the three theories help us to decide which was the more significant?

ACTIVITY 1: COMMENTARY

(A) HOW WOULD THE THREE ETHICAL THEORIES CLARIFY OUR DECISION IN THIS CONFLICT?

What would a utilitarian have to say about the criterion of the extent of need?

- A utilitarian is going to be particularly interested in how we see the extent of need. Do we mean 'how many people are in need?' or 'what is the extent of people's need?' or both? If there are lots of people at starvation level, then there could be considerable increases in well-being if this was relieved. If the percentage of those in need who are starving is very low, then the increases in well-being might not be so dramatically high.

- To the extent that there is need (however we define it), an increased satisfaction of these needs would increase previously needy people's preferences. This could be detailed in terms of less malnutrition, more education, better health, better accommodation, and so on.

- To the extent that need (however we define it) has been reduced, those who have given for this purpose might feel greater well-being.

- Of course, at least some of those who have given might have less well-being. This could be (looking ahead to Nozick) that they had no choice in the giving. If the need-reduction has been achieved by governments giving money (and other resources) paid for out of taxation, the libertarians will very likely have their well-being reduced. This would also apply if banks had cancelled debts, and then passed the cost of doing so on to their customers.

- The evidence of public opinion would be relevant in assessing the previous two points.

What would a deontologist have to say about the criterion of the extent of need?

- If we take a Kantian position that we should value autonomy, then (as we have seen) we have a duty to ensure that people's autonomy is preserved. People in considerable need cannot have autonomy. In this way, since the extent of need can be seen as the extent of non-autonomy, this criterion has to be accepted.

- If we join Rawls behind the veil of ignorance, then any level of need that we would not tolerate has to be unacceptable. In this way, the extent of need is a very important criterion.

- If we use the difference principle of Rawls, then the extent of need remains of central concern. We have seen that this principle allows inequality as long as the most unequal benefit most from this arrangement. Thus the extent of need has to be on the agenda. Those who are the poorest in the world (in the most need) would have to benefit from the present distribution of global resources more than others for us not to put it as a very important criterion.

What would a libertarian have to say about the criterion of the extent of need?

- The criterion of the extent of need is always going to be a problem for the libertarian, if we are talking about the extent of other people's need. Nozick might hand over some of his resources to help to reduce the extent of need, but he is not required to take this criterion into account.

So far we have considered that the criterion of the extent of need would fit with both the utilitarian and the deontological positions, but would not fit well with the libertarian one. What about the criterion of the nature of the regime?

What would a utilitarian have to say about the criterion of the nature of the regime?

- The utilitarian would have to be concerned that, unless we take the nature of the regime into account, any potential increase in well-being from giving financial help might not be maximised.

- If it could be shown that much of the financial help would be siphoned off through corruption, then the utilitarian would want to consider the reduced well-being of those who have given the aid. Knowing that this money ends lining the pockets of corrupt officials would lead to a reduction of well-being virtually all round. (The exception is obviously those who benefit from the corruption.)

What would a deontologist have to say about the criterion of the nature of the regime?

- The deontologist has the same problem as the utilitarian with the nature of the regime.

If the nature of the regime is such that it prevents assistance producing the desired result, then the autonomy that the Kantian is seeking will not be produced. In this way, the nature of the regime has a great significance to this position.

- Rawls will be seeking to produce justice. If the nature of the regime gets in the way of producing (something like) this, then the nature of the regime is of great significance in determining how we should act. Either from behind the veil of ignorance or using the difference principle, we find that the nature of the regime is relevant to the problem of how we should relieve poverty in developing countries.

What would a libertarian have to say about the criterion of the nature of the regime?

- The nature of the regime is also significant for the libertarian. At an important level, the libertarian will always find corrupt and repressive regimes unacceptable. They take what is not theirs to take. (Although, of course, they will find any government unacceptable because of this.) In this way, the libertarian will have to see the nature of the regime as of great significance to decisions in this area.

- The nature of the regime will take on a particular significance to the libertarian if the money to help reduce need has been given freely. If I give to help the poor in developing countries, then I will be ethically enraged if this gift is stolen by those to whom it was not given.

So what do the ethical theories tell us about using these two criteria together?

All three positions are going to see the nature of the regime as a criterion that has to be included in decision-making. Until it is taken into account, then the criterion of the extent of need cannot be used fully. The utilitarian cannot seek to usefully increase well-being; the deontologist cannot usefully increase autonomy, or justify inequality; the libertarian cannot allow the theft of property.

Given these considerations, where would this importance of the nature of the regime lead us on the continuum of choice? Position (6) emerges as one that might appeal to all of the ethical theories. Position (8) is the same (with some provisos). For the libertarian, position (1) to (3) could have some appeal, given the intention of having property restored to those who rightly own it. (Having got the property back, it could then be freely given to those in need, without giving it to the corrupt regime.) For the utilitarian and the deontologist any of the positions could be justified if we could show that they would result in greater well-being or autonomy. But we have seen that, given that the nature of the regime is likely to get in the way of this being achieved, some of the positions are not easy to defend. For example, positions (5), (9), and (10) are all problematic because of this.

(B) WHAT ABOUT THE CRITERIA OF COST AND PUBLIC OPINION?

What would a utilitarian have to say about the criteria of cost and public opinion?

• It is clear that a utilitarian cannot ignore public opinion. If a particular decision conflicted with public opinion, then it is likely to lead to a reduction in well-being.

• However, we need to consider what we mean by 'public opinion'. Do we include only that of people in the donor nations or do we also include that of people in countries that will receive aid? Do we have to look at how keenly opinions are held? If I don't really worry too much about making poverty history, but you care very much that we should give as much as we can, does this mean your well-being is more important than mine? And what about my Nozickean neighbour who cares just as deeply as you, but her position is that money should not be taken from her in order to help others?

• Cost comes into the utilitarian framework as an issue that demands our attention by asking us whether the price of debt-relief can be justified. The utilitarian would have to ask the general question 'Does the spending of money on debt-relief achieve the greatest level of welfare?' Specific questions could emerge from this general one. For example, 'Could we spend the money in different ways that would maximise welfare?'

The Commission for Africa has asked for an extra $25 billion a year between 2008-2010. This seems to be a huge amount of money. But it amounts to only 0.08% of the 22 richest donor countries, GDP. In addition, the European Union spent $55 billion in 2004 keeping farmers' incomes artificially high[2]. So, could we argue that the extra $25 billion a year could easily be afforded without there being a noticeable reduction in welfare for rich countries, but a big increase in the welfare of people in poor countries?

What would a deontologist have to say about the criteria of cost and public opinion?

• Does an emphasis on the ethics of duty cut through the possible conflict between cost and public opinion? In an important way, yes. Our duty to help people be autonomous and to act justly is not constrained by public opinion. It is a duty that cannot be rejected even if, say, 56% of the population aren't in favour of spending money to help. The cost could indeed be justified if what was spent led to less injustice (more autonomy). Of course, if the amount that was given meant that we couldn't satisfy the need to act justly in our own country, then there could be a problem. For example, if the Government said to the people of a poor inner-city area 'You can't have your new hospital that would undoubtedly save lives because we've given this money to fund a new factory in Zimbabwe', then the people in this area could protest. (Think of how they could do it from each of the three ethical positions.)

What would a libertarian have to say about the criteria of cost and public opinion?

• The libertarian is on comfortable ground here. Of course you can't sacrifice public opinion on the altar of ethical duty to others. If debt-relief costs the public money, and they haven't specifically consented to paying for debt-relief, then we would have to look at public opinion. When a charity says that 'what you should give is just the equivalent of a cup of coffee a week', our Nozickean citizen reminds the charity 'Yes, but it's my cup of coffee'.

So where have we got to with putting cost and public opinion together?

If spending whatever money is necessary leads to an overall increase in well-being, then the utilitarian will sleep easily in their bed tonight. If public opinion is not in support of spending this money, then they would have to stay awake fretting about a possible reduction in the public's well-being (depending, as we have seen, on how keenly this is felt, how many people feel like this, the improvements of welfare in poor countries, and so on). Cost is therefore justified in terms of outcome.

For the deontologist, there is less of a problem to trouble their sleep. If public opinion is against helping the poor in developing countries, then there remains a duty to help (via Kant's emphasis on autonomy or Rawls' emphasis on acting according to principles of justice).

For the libertarian, if public opinion is against giving aid, then those who are against it cannot be ignored. Their opinion is central to the decision as to what to do.

REFERENCES

(1) P A Fortes and E L Zoboli, 'A study on the ethics of microallocation of scarce resources in health care', *Journal of Medical Ethics*, August 2002, pp. 266–269

(2) 'Helping Africa help itself', *The Economist*, July 2 2005, p. 11

PART II / UNIT 4
CRITICAL REASONING

INTRODUCTION: WHAT IS THIS UNIT CONCERNED WITH?

If we look at the skills that are developed by Critical Thinking, we find that the list we would expect to find at AS level is the same as that at A2 level. At one level, this might be surprising. At another level, it isn't.

Because Critical Thinking is very much concerned with the development and practice of skills, we would expect that skills learned in one year would be built upon in the second. It is this 'building on' that is particularly important. Someone who learns how to dance, or skate, or play chess doesn't leave the early skills behind when they move on to higher levels of skill. Even with driving a car, there are opportunities once you've passed your driving test to do an advanced driving test in order to refine and develop your skills.

The skills that were (or should have been) developed by an AS course are the following:

- Analysing arguments
- Drawing inferences
- Identifying assumptions
- Evaluating evidence (looking at facts and judgements)
- Evaluating reasoning
- Identifying and explaining flaws in an argument
- Assessing the credibility of documents and other sources
- Evaluating analogies
- Evaluating definitions
- Evaluating hypotheses
- Identifying, evaluating, and applying principles

- Examining meaning in context
- Understanding explanations
- Recognising and producing counter-arguments
- Producing further arguments

Except for credibility of documents (which featured very strongly in Unit 1 of the AS), all of the above skills will continue to be developed in the A2.

What we can expect is that the skills will be raised to higher levels of performance through working with a range of more difficult material. We'll start doing this in the next chapter.

6
UNRAVELLING COMPLEXITY

We know that an argument must always contain at least something that is recognisable as R → C. We also know that arguments will often contain more than one reason, and sometimes more than one conclusion. Beyond these basics, you will have come across arguments that contain counter-arguments or -claims, that include what we can call 'scene-setting' material, and that include material that might not be relevant to the argument as such.

In looking to unravel complexity, we need to be clear what is going in arguments. Some of these arguments can be short but densely packed with argumentation. Others will be longer, with a looser structure which sometimes fails to hold together.

In that we're building upon existing skills, there's always a good argument for practising what we have done before. Unusually then, we're going to begin with an activity.

ACTIVITY 1

Read the following passage. In reading it, try to work out how the argument develops. You will obviously need to be looking for reasons and conclusions, but you should also look at what other parts of the passage are doing.

LETHAL BULLETS COMING THROUGH THE WATER

When species are moved out of one environment into another, most of them either die or fail to flourish. However, some species thrive in their different environment and can even go on to become a problem for it. An example of the latter is the grey squirrel. This was introduced into Britain from the US at the end of the nineteenth century and has become widespread in England and Wales. It has contributed to the decline of the red squirrel in this country.

A further example is the zebra mussel. This is native to Eastern Europe but has appeared in the waters of North America. The mussels were probably introduced into the Great Lakes in 1985 by sea-going ships coming from Europe. Its numbers have grown hugely since that time. The zebra mussel is now a major problem for both other wildlife and for the economy. They eat the plankton that other animals need, effectively starving juvenile fish to death. They also do millions of dollars-worth of damage by blocking water-intake pipes of drinking-water facilities, power-station water pipes, and those of other industrial facilities. Solving the problem is an urgent need.

Zebra mussels can present a health hazard by increasing human exposure to organic pollutants such as PCBs and PAHs. This is because they accumulate pollutants in their tissues in concentrations that can be 300,000 times greater than we find in the environment. They deposit these pollutants as loose pellets of mucous, which can then be eaten by other animals and passed up the food chain. Furthermore the mussels can provide a different sort of health hazard on bathing beaches, in that bathers can cut their feet on the sharp edges of their shells.

There have been various attempts to get rid of the mussels. Chlorine is effective against them, but unfortunately it's bad for all other wildlife. It's also bad for humans, in that it tends to react with natural compounds to form those that can cause cancer. Chilli powder and electrocution might be less of a problem, and have both been used, but they're not as effective as chlorine.

However, an answer to the problem might be available. Potassium chloride is a lethal chemical in sufficiently high concentrations. (It's used as part of the cocktail of drugs in lethal injections in US executions.) However, in low concentrations it is harmless.

Dr David Aldridge of Cambridge University has developed a way of delivering the potassium chloride to the mussels without causing harm to other species. This is done by putting very small amounts of the chemical inside coatings of fatty acids. These are then put into water pipes clogged by the mussels. The mussels filter these and digest them. The mussels are poisoned by this concentration of potassium chloride, but any uneaten pellets are dissolved safely in the water.

By being both effective and safe, this method seems to have all that is required to attack the problem of zebra mussels. It is to be hoped that Dr Aldridge's 'biobullets' will soon be shooting their way towards them.

If you have now completed Activity 1, you will have practised your skills in seeing which parts of a passage are the argument itself, and which parts perform other functions such as what we can call 'scene-setting' and explanation. We'll keep coming back to such points as we look at further material.

Before we do this, we're going to have a look at specific types of argument. Before now, we haven't worried about how the form of an argument can affect a judgement of it. We've just looked at the relationship between reasons and conclusions, paying attention to their sequence and whether the conclusion is sufficiently supported by the reason(s).

There is, however, an area of analysis of argument in which the form of the argument is of central importance. We will look at this now.

FORM AND CONTENT

When we show the structure of an argument as an R → C form, we are isolating those parts of an argument that fit into this structure. We don't show explanations, scene-setting, or examples in the structure. But, even in this distilled form, we haven't shown much of the relationship between the reasons and the conclusion(s). A good argument (one in which the conclusion is not overdrawn) will look the same as a poor argument (one in which the conclusion is overdrawn) when we present it in this way.

Some arguments, however, will reveal either strength or weakness if reduced to the bare bones of their form. In this section, we're going to look at examples in which the form will either reveal the strength or it will show its weakness.

You will sometimes see the term **syllogism** used when looking at particular types of argument. The term can be used loosely or even wrongly[1]. To simplify what is meant by the term, the first thing to note is that a syllogism consists of two reasons which together lead to the conclusion. It is, however, more than this. Each reason in a syllogism has one term in common with the conclusion, and one term in common with the other reason. An example should clarify this.

R(1): All hard-working students are good at Critical Thinking.

R(2): All students who are good at Critical Thinking have read at least one book by Roy van den Brink-Budgen.

C: So all hard-working students have read at least one book by Roy van den Brink-Budgen.

You can see that the conclusion does not contain what is called the 'middle term' which is 'students who are good at Critical Thinking'. But you can see how the conclusion is drawn from the content of the two reasons.

Syllogisms come in various forms. We'll meet some of them below.

DILEMMAS: REAL AND FALSE

We spent a lot of time in Unit 3 looking at dilemmas. You will remember that, faced with a dilemma, we were concerned with having to decide between two options (that we had narrowed down from many more). We meet dilemmas again here when we're looking at the structure of an argument. We're also going to meet various technical terms that we haven't met before.

Look at the next argument.

> *Either the Leader of the Opposition is telling the truth that there are no links between his party and the property developing company 'Skyscrape UK' or he is deliberately misinforming the public. It cannot be that he would risk lying about this link (in case he was ever found out to have done so), so he must be telling the truth.*

This argument starts with a dilemma: either the Leader of the Opposition is telling the truth or he is not. Then there is a premise or reason given in order to draw the conclusion. Before we say more about this type of reasoning, let's be sure we can see what the form of the argument is.

If we give the letters A and B for the components of the argument, we can see that it has the following form.

> *Either (A) the Leader of the Opposition is telling the truth that there are no links between his party and the property developing company 'Skyscrape UK' or (B) he is deliberately misinforming the public. (Not B) It cannot be that he would risk lying about this link (in case he was ever found out to have done so), so (A) he must be telling the truth.*

Put very baldly, the structure is

A or B
Not B
Therefore A

The same thing is going on in the next argument.

> *Either the Government will have to risk unpopularity by putting up taxes to pay for*
> *people to draw pensions by the age of 65, or we have to expect to work beyond that*
> *age (to 68 or more). The Government can't afford to risk being unpopular as a*
> *result of putting up taxes for this purpose, so people will have to work beyond 65.*

The structure amounts to the same, though there is one difference.

A or B
Not A
Therefore B

The difference is unimportant. The order in which the alternatives are presented does not affect the nature of the argument.

This form of argument is an example of what is called a **deductive** argument. We can go further and say that arguments of this type are **deductively valid** in that, if their reasons are true, the conclusion has to also be true. You can see why. If it is true that we have (only) either option A or B, and if one option is not the case/is unacceptable, the other one must be the case/acceptable.

Technically, what we have in this case is what's called a 'disjunctive syllogism'. This is because the 'either A or B' statement is called a disjunction.

But what if there is a problem, not with the form, but with the content? The most obvious way in which there could be a problem with the content is if there is more than A or B to choose from. In other words, the dilemma we saw in the above arguments isn't a dilemma with only these two choices. There could be C or D or …

In this case, the conclusion is problematic because the reasons are not correct. This is an example of what is called a **false dilemma**. We met this in the book for the AS course on pages 103-104 where we looked at the problem in an argument of restricting the options (and in this book on page 2). Faced with the above argument about pensions, for example, we could say that other options could be 'we could reduce the level of pension paid at 65, but still allow people to retire at that age' or 'we could encourage more people to pay into private pension schemes so that they can retire at 65'.

But if we are satisfied that the reasons given do not amount to a false dilemma and that they are therefore correct, then the conclusion must follow and the argument must then be valid.

A clear example is this argument.

> *The police said yesterday that, within twenty-four hours, they would either charge the woman with murder or release her without charge. She was seen being dropped off at her house by a police car this afternoon. So she has not been charged with murder.*

The structure is as before.

Either A or B
Not A
Therefore B

If the police correctly presented the two options that they had, then the conclusion must follow. The argument is deductively valid.

IMPLICATION

There are other forms of argument that are deductively valid. Implication is one of them. This has a structure which has a hypothetical form.

> *If we put up taxes to pay for people to draw their pension at the age of 65, then people won't have to work beyond that age. Taxes in fact are going to be increased to pay for people to be able to draw their pensions at 65, so people won't have to work beyond that age.*

The structure of this argument can be given as follows.

If A is true, then B is true.
A is true.
So B is true.

In such arguments, A is called the antecedent and B is called the consequent. There will always be two reasons and a conclusion.

R(1): If we put up taxes to pay for people to draw their pension at the age of 65, then people won't have to work beyond that age.

R(2): Taxes are going to be increased to pay for people to be able to draw their pensions at 65.

C: So people won't have to work beyond that age.

The reasons have to include a statement that the truth of one thing is dependent on the truth of something else (as in R(1)). When the antecedent is shown to be true, then the consequent has to be also (because of the structure of the argument).

Implication is therefore a form of argument which is deductively valid. Those of you who like to use technical terms might like to refer to this form of argument by its other name which is *modus ponens*. This means 'mode (of argument) that affirms'. You can see why: we are affirming (stating as a fact) that A is true. You can see why this form of argument is also referred to as 'affirming the antecedent'.

We need to be careful, however, that we haven't mistaken a different form of argument for implication. The next type of argument structure has perhaps a deceptive appeal.

AFFIRMING THE CONSEQUENT

As we have seen, implication gives us an argument that is deductively valid. Any argument that has the form of implication will have a conclusion that is true if the reasons it is drawn from are also true. But a shift in the structure can produce a very different result.

If we put up taxes to pay for people to draw their pension at the age of 65, then people won't have to work beyond that age. People won't have to work beyond the age of 65, so taxes must be going up.

This has the following structure.

If A is true, then B is true.
B is true.
So A is true.

This form of argument is not deductively valid. The truth of A does not depend on the truth of B: it is the other way round. The relationship between A and B cannot simply be reversed as if the order of the argument doesn't matter. There could be other reasons why people won't have to work beyond the age of 65. Perhaps lots of people have joined private pension schemes which will reduce the need for the State to pay people's pensions at the early age of 65.

The next two examples further highlight the crucial difference between implication and affirming the consequent.

If you study this book well, then you will pass the A2 exam in Critical Thinking with a good grade. You have clearly studied this book well. So you will pass the A2 exam with a good grade.

If you study this book well, then you will pass the A2 exam in Critical Thinking with a good grade. You have passed the A2 exam with an A grade. So you must have studied this book well.

You will have seen that the first example is a deductively valid argument. The truth of B depended on the truth of A. The truth of A was established, so that of B was also shown. The second example affirmed the consequent, so is not a valid form of argument. The truth of A did not depend on the truth of B, so the conclusion about the truth of A could not be drawn. (You could, for example, have been very well taught, so well done to your teacher. You could have read a different book? And got an A? Not likely is it?)

CHAIN ARGUMENTS

We have so far looked at two forms of deductively valid arguments (and one invalid one). Now we're going to look at a third valid form.

Chain arguments are sometimes called *hypothetical syllogisms*. They are an extension to the type of hypothetical form that we saw in implication. In a chain argument, another link (so to speak) is added to the sequence of the argument.

Here is an example.

If global warming is taking place, then we can expect sea levels to rise. If sea levels rise, huge areas of our coastline will disappear. So, if global warming is taking place, we can expect widespread flooding of much of our coastline.

You can see why this form of argument is called 'chain argument'. The structure makes clear the links between the beginning and the end.

If A, then B
If B, then C
So, if A, then C

The truth of C comes from the truth of B, whose truth comes from A.

Problems can arise in chain arguments when the form of the argument appears to be that of a chain, but when at least one link is broken by a shift in the meaning of the terms that are used. It is clear that if we are using A, B, and C to refer to statements, then the statements must be equivalent. Where they are not, we have the problem of **equivocation**. In this problem, the author takes two (or more) terms to mean the same thing, though they do not.

> *When we look at petrol prices in other countries, we find that motorists in the UK pay more for their fuel than those in these other countries, especially those in the US (where prices are about a third of those in the UK). But, if petrol prices weren't so high, then more people would use their vehicles for inessential journeys. If that were to happen, then the environment would suffer from vehicle emissions much more than it already does. Thus, if the costs of motoring in the UK weren't about the highest in the world, then the environment would suffer more than it already does from traffic.*

Though this argument has a look of a chain argument, the author has taken one part of the argument as if it's equivalent to another. This is 'if petrol prices weren't so high' and 'if the costs of motoring in the UK weren't about the highest in the world'. Though the two are similar, they're not equivalent. The cost of petrol is only one part of the cost of motoring (other parts include the cost of the vehicles themselves, the cost of insurance, road tax, and so on).

DENYING THE CONSEQUENT

We looked above at an invalid form of argument which is called 'affirming the consequent'. We now look at a valid form of argument called 'denying the consequent'. This is sometimes referred to by its Latin name of *modus tollens*. Just as *modus ponens* meant 'mode that affirms', this means 'mode that denies'. We shall see why. In some ways, arguments of this type can look problematic rather than valid.

If Hannie is hungry, then she couldn't have eaten breakfast. But we know she did eat breakfast. So Hannie can't be hungry.

The structure of this argument is as follows.

If A, then B
Not B
Therefore not A

This has a look of the invalid form of argument 'affirming the consequent' (if A, then B, B is true, therefore A). But the crucial difference is that the consequent (B) is denied rather than affirmed.

As with all the other forms of valid argument that we have considered, the truth of the conclusion requires the truth of the reasons. Thus the relationship between the antecedent and the consequent needs to be such that the only way for the consequent to be true is for the antecedent to be true. If we could deny the consequent without there being any significance for the antecedent, then this argument form would not be valid.

If the police are going to be able to reduce organised crime, then they need to infiltrate the various gangs that commit the crime. They haven't been able to infiltrate these gangs, so they're not going to be able to reduce organised crime.

This argument has the right structure for a valid argument. What would make it a problem would be if there are ways that the police are going to be able to reduce organised crime that don't involve infiltrating the gangs. For example, they could get some gang members to 'grass' on those higher up in exchange for shorter sentences (as is done in the US). In this example, then, the reason isn't true, so neither is the conclusion.

We also need to watch out for arguments in which it is the antecedent that is denied rather than the consequent. The next argument is an example of this.

If the police are going to be able to reduce organised crime, then they need to infiltrate the various gangs that commit the crime. The police aren't going to be able to reduce organised crime, so they haven't been able to infiltrate these various gangs.

If A, then B
Not A (A is not true)
So not B (B is not true)

You can see that denying the antecedent is not a valid form of argument. In the above example, the police could have infiltrated various gangs even though they can't reduce organised crime.

ACTIVITY 2[2]

What is the structure of each of the following arguments?
Which of them is deductively valid?

(1)

Japan has the second largest defence spending in the world (after the US). This can mean only one of two things. One is that Japan intends to become the second most important military nation in the world. The other is that they are spending such a large amount in order to counteract the importance of China in that part of the world. Given that Japan and China have historically been enemies, the second of these is clearly the case. It follows that Japan is not interested in becoming the second most important military nation in the world.

(2)

The last census in this country was in 2001, with the next one due (as always, ten years later, in 2011). There was, however, a problem with the last census. This is that the census figure for the UK population was 1.1 million lower than the population estimate for 2001. The particular problem was that the number of males between the ages of 15 and 35 was too low. Explanations for the problem included some of these young men not bothering to fill in the census forms, and some of them being foreign and so not thinking that the form applied to them. There is also the probability that some of them were living with young women who were claiming single parent benefit and so kept quiet about where they lived. There is also the possibility, of course, that the population estimate itself was too high. So, if the estimate was too high, then the census figure was accurate. But the census figure can't have been right because it makes no sense for London boroughs to lose population 'overnight'. It must be that the prediction of the size of the UK population is the reliable figure.

(3)

For ten years, four out of five adults in the UK have seen the gap between rich and poor as too large. However, only two out of five agree that the government should do something about closing the gap. This must show that people either think that the poor should work harder to close the gap or that they think that wages of poorer people should be raised to help to close the gap. Raising the level of wages at the bottom end isn't popular with other workers so we must conclude that people think that it is up to the poor to work harder.

(4)

The UK is the second biggest consumer of chocolate per head in the world (after, perhaps not surprisingly, Switzerland). We consume fewer vegetables than the world average. There are some countries (Greece and Turkey are examples) that eat more than two and half times as many vegetables as we do. This evidence suggests that, if we are looking at ways of improving the diet of the UK population, we need to discourage people from eating so much chocolate and encourage them to eat far more vegetables. If such a policy worked, we would see considerable benefits to health. Therefore we should have such a policy.

(5)

Over half of the population in the UK has less than £1500 in savings, with at least half of these having no savings at all. Perhaps not surprisingly, the amount of savings a household has reflects one thing in particular. This is whether there are dependent children in the household. If there are, then savings are likely to be below £10,000. Eighty-two per cent of couples with dependent children fall into this category. Things are even worse for single parents with dependent children, with only three per cent of these having savings of more than £10,000. If the amount of savings is a measure of people's financial health, then at least 50 per cent of the population is suffering financial ill-health. If this percentage has these financial problems, we need to encourage people, particularly those with dependent children, to save. In this way, if the amount of savings is a guide to people's financial well-being, we need to encourage people (especially households with dependent children) to save.

(6)

We are often told that what is called 'alternative' or 'complementary' medicine is more effective than conventional medicine at treating many disorders. For example, what are called chiropractors claim to be able to treat neck and back pain. If it is the case that 'alternative' medicine is more effective than conventional medicine at *treating many disorders, then those who practise it should be able to give us evidence that shows this to be true. As it is, there is no such evidence. For example, recent evidence on chiropractic showed that it was not effective for any condition. Therefore we can conclude that 'alternative' medicine is not more effective than conventional medicine.*

(7)

We are often told that what is called 'alternative' or 'complementary medicine' is more effective than conventional medicine at treating many disorders. For example, homeopaths claim to be able to treat illnesses by minute doses of substances that in undiluted forms would be poisonous. If 'alternative' medicine works, then it would save the National Health Service (NHS) a lot of money (in that the treatments can often be fairly cheap). If 'alternative' medicine will save the NHS a lot of money, then we should welcome such medicine. Therefore we should welcome it.

(8)

Accident statistics reveal that the fatal road accident rate for motorcyclists has gone up substantially since the 1990s. If fatal accident rates for other road users (including pedestrians) had not increased since that time, then we could claim that various road safety programmes had been at least partly successful. Interestingly, it is the case that only motorcyclists have seen their fatal accident increase since the 1990s. As a result, we can say that programmes to improve road safety have been in some ways successful.

FROM CERTAINTY TO PROBABILITY

When looking at **deductive arguments**, we have seen that we can draw conclusions with certainty. But we could draw them with certainty only if the reasons are true. If they are not, then the truth of the conclusion suffers accordingly.

If Ipswich is the greatest football team, then they will defeat any other team. Ipswich is the greatest football team, so they will win every match.

Though the argument has the form of a deductive argument (implication), the conclusion cannot be drawn because unfortunately (though some might have sung this on many occasions) Ipswich is not the greatest football team (yet).

The question of the truth of the reasons is in this way important for the quality of the argument. Most arguments that we come across are not deductive. They are what is called 'inductive'. With inductive arguments, we are looking at the probability of the conclusion being true. This does not mean that with inductive arguments the reasons aren't true. It's that, even if they are, the conclusion need not be. You will have read many such arguments when you studied for the AS course. It's what you're used to seeing.

You might remember that in my book *Critical Thinking for AS Level* we looked at the question of the strength of arguments (pages 91-93). We looked particularly at how conclusions need to be limited to what the reasoning allows. This is particularly the case when we are looking at statistical evidence.

To remind yourself of this point, do the next exercise.

ACTIVITY 3

In a study in the US, it was shown that the proportion of women taking their husband's name on marriage has increased. In the US study, 23 per cent of college-educated women in 1990 kept their own surname on marriage; in 2000, the figure was only 17 per cent. Why this is so is likely to have something to do with social change in the US. It has been suggested that, unlike in 1990, marriage in the US now confers a status that women in their late 20s or early 30s might want to have, and the change of name might represent a symbol of that status. Whatever the reasons, it is interesting to note that, in the UK, no research has been done into the percentage of women keeping their surname. The suggestion is that in the UK women have not seen giving up their surname as significant. This is because they have seen themselves as equals with their husbands, and so haven't needed to make statements about independence.

Which one of the following is an inference which can safely be drawn from the above passage?

(A) Unlike in the UK, many women in the US marry in order to achieve a higher status.

(B) Women in the US increasingly see marriage in a similar way to how women in the UK see it.

(C)   Women in the UK who keep their own surname upon marriage do this for different reasons than those of women in the US.

(D)   The choice of name a woman uses after marriage in both the US and the UK could be seen as having symbolic significance.

What this exercise shows is that the inference we drew was one which fitted with the information in the passage. The others could not be supported by this information: they went beyond what it allowed. Though we can defend our answer in this way and show why it can be drawn more safely than the others, in the end we are looking for an inference which has a probability of being true. This probability contrasts with the certainty of the conclusions which were drawn in deductive arguments. This point is given emphasis by the tentative nature of the explanation for women in the US now taking their husbands' name. The generally limited nature of the evidence gives further emphasis to the conclusion being no more than its being probably correct.

It is possible that further evidence could be provided which would challenge this conclusion. An obvious example would be evidence on women in the UK, especially as we are told that 'no research has been done on the percentage of women keeping their surname'.

We'll have a look at another exercise to see how an inductive argument works.

> The 'Make Poverty History' campaign of 2005 stressed that all that was needed to achieve this was to do three things. These were to ensure 'trade justice', 'to drop the debt', and to provide 'more and better aid'. The first of these was contrasted with 'free trade'. The evidence, however, is all against getting rid of free trade. If trade justice is what's needed, then free trade must be protected. Keeping tariffs on trade results in unproductive use of resources, such as farming. Free trade allows resources to be used much more productively. There are plenty of examples. Malaysia, India, and South Korea were poor countries in the 1980s. Since the getting rid of restrictions on trade, their economies have flourished. Even Oxfam can see it. They argue that, if Africa could increase its share of world trade by just one per cent, it would earn another £49 billion a year. Unrestricted trade with the rest of the world would encourage investment and allow in cheap imports.

Which one of the following is the best statement of the **main conclusion** of the above argument?

(A)   Free trade would attract investment and allow cheap imports, both of which would benefit Africa.

(B)   Free trade is necessary if trade justice is what is needed.

(C)   The evidence on what happens when tariffs on trade are allowed shows that resources are used unproductively.

(D)   Free trade allows resources to be used much more productively than with trade tariffs.

The structure of this argument has a familiar look to it. The author presents a counter-position (the first three sentences) and then begins their argument (with the word 'however' showing that). The conclusion appears shortly afterwards in a hypothetical form ('if trade justice ....'). What follows are reasons for this conclusion. The answer is therefore (B).

In looking at this structure we could see that the author was giving various reasons, with evidence provided to support them. This use of evidence highlights how the conclusion is drawn as no more than a probable (rather than a certain) conclusion. The use of Malaysia, India, and South Korea are given as examples of countries whose 'economies have flourished' following 'the getting rid of restrictions'. If there are counter-examples, then the author's argument is weakened. In addition, if we could show that 'keeping tariffs on trade' leads to productive use of resources, then again we have weakened the argument.

We could put the above argument into a deductively valid form in many ways. The following is one of them.

> *If we want to achieve 'trade justice' in the world, then countries must be allowed to develop their economies without restrictions. If countries are allowed such an unrestricted development of their economies, then free trade between them is necessary. Therefore, if we want to achieve 'trade justice', then free trade between countries is necessary.*

You will see that this is in the form of a chain argument. As we have seen, if the reasons are true, then the conclusion ('if we want to achieve "trade justice", then free trade between countries is necessary') must be true, given the form of the argument.

The inductive version of this argument does not require its conclusion to be drawn. It is a conclusion that fits, that follows, that is relevant. But it's not a conclusion that is necessary, given the reasons. The author could have drawn different conclusions.

The 'Make Poverty History' campaign should look at different ways of achieving their aim.

The ways by which Malaysia, India, and South Korea have achieved economic success are available to all countries.

The deductive form of the argument could not have led to a different conclusion without moving beyond its structure into an inductive form.

ACTIVITY 4

What is the main conclusion of this argument?
What other conclusions could the author have drawn?

Between 2003-2008, there is predicted to be a huge growth in the sales of organic food. In the UK, this will be an increase of 77 per cent, with similarly high figures for other countries. This predicted massive growth is to be regretted. The UK Food Standards Agency says that there is nothing wrong with using low levels of pesticides in producing food. In this country we use only low levels. This is just as well, because the Soil Association (which strongly supports organic food) accepts that organic farmers can use seven pesticides. Various claims are made about organic food but, as the Soil Association admits, there is little, if any, evidence to support them. Indeed, the Association has been told that they cannot, in their advertising, claim that organic farming produces healthier food and that it is more humane to animals. Why? Because they can't prove either claim. However, what is not in dispute is that organic food is indeed different in one important way: it's more expensive.

What we have seen in this chapter is that the simple description of arguments as reasons that support conclusions is one that, though accurate, obscures the differences between types of arguments. But what we can stress is that, whatever the form of the argument, the question of the truth of the reasons is always there. The difference is that, with deductive arguments, the truth of the reasons guarantees (requires) the truth of the conclusion. With inductive arguments, the reasons could be true even though the conclusion is no more than (at best) probably true.

ACTIVITY 1: COMMENTARY

We will look at this passage in detail to see what's going on at each stage.

When species are moved out of one environment into another, most of them either die or fail to flourish. However, some species thrive in their different environment and can even go on to become a problem for it. An example of the latter is the grey squirrel. This was introduced into Britain from the US at the end of the nineteenth century and has become widespread in England and Wales. It has contributed to the decline of the red squirrel in this country.

What has happened so far?

The author has made a general claim (the first sentence) and then a claim that there are exceptions to it (second sentence). What follows is an example of such an exception, showing both that the grey squirrel has thrived in a different environment and that it has been a problem. Obviously no argument has happened yet.

A further example is the zebra mussel. This is native to Eastern Europe but has appeared in the waters of North America. The mussels were probably introduced into the Great Lakes in 1985 by sea-going ships coming from Europe. Its numbers have grown hugely since that time. The zebra mussel is now a major problem for both other wildlife and for the economy. They eat the plankton that other animals need, effectively starving juvenile fish to death. They also do millions of dollars-worth of damage by blocking water-intake pipes of drinking-water facilities, power-station water pipes, and those of other industrial facilities. Solving the problem is an urgent need.

Has the passage progressed into an argument yet?

The author does the same thing with the zebra mussel as they did with the grey squirrel. They give evidence to show that the mussel has thrived in its new environment and provide an explanation of why it is a problem in this environment. Has the author yet given an argument? Let's look at this evidence and explanation in a different order.

R(1): Zebra mussels eat the plankton that other animals need, effectively starving juvenile fish to death.

R(2): They also do millions of dollars-worth of damage by blocking water-intake pipes of drinking-water facilities, power-station water pipes, and those of other industrial facilities.

C: The zebra mussel is now a major problem for both other wildlife and for the economy.

We can now see the information as providing support for the conclusion that (therefore) the zebra mussel is now a major problem. The two reasons are independent reasons in that each provides a separate support for the conclusion.

Of course, you will have noted that the author had done more than this. They had also said that 'solving the problem is an urgent need'. The argument has in this way moved on. You should be able to see what this does to the structure so far.

R(1) + R(2) → IC (The zebra mussel is now a major problem) → C (Solving the problem is an urgent need.)

The passage continues.

Zebra mussels can present a health hazard by increasing human exposure to organic pollutants such as PCBs and PAHs. This is because they accumulate pollutants in their tissues in concentrations that can be 300,000 times greater than we find in the environment. They deposit these pollutants as loose pellets of mucous, which can then be eaten by other animals and passed up the food chain. Furthermore the mussels can provide a different sort of health hazard on bathing beaches in that bathers can cut their feet on the sharp edges of their shells.

What has happened to the argument now? We have two further reasons why we need to solve the problem of the zebra mussel.

R(3): Zebra mussels can present a health hazard by increasing human exposure to organic pollutants such as PCBs and PAHs.

R(4): The mussels can provide a different sort of health hazard on bathing beaches in that bathers can cut their feet on the sharp edges of their shells.

So the structure is now

R(1) + R(2) → IC + R(3) + R(4) → C

We also have an explanation of how the mussels present a health hazard via pollution, and how they create a different hazard on bathing beaches.

The passage continues.

> *There have been various attempts to get rid of the mussels. Chlorine is effective against them, but unfortunately it's bad for all other wildlife. It's also bad for humans, in that it tends to react with natural compounds to form those that can cause cancer. Chilli powder and electrocution might be less of a problem, and have both been used, but they're not as effective as chlorine.*

Has the argument progressed? No, not as an argument. The author has so far concluded that the problem of zebra mussels needs solving urgently. What the above tells us is that attempts to solve the problem are either insufficiently effective or create other problems.

> *However, an answer to the problem might be available. Potassium chloride is a lethal chemical in sufficiently high concentrations. (It's used as part of the cocktail of drugs in lethal injections in US executions.) However, in low concentrations it is harmless.*

> *Dr David Aldridge of Cambridge University has developed a way of delivering the potassium chloride to the mussels without causing harm to other species. This is done by putting very small amounts of the chemical inside coatings of fatty acids. These are then put into water pipes clogged by the mussels. The mussels filter these and digest them. The mussels are poisoned by this concentration of potassium chloride, but any uneaten pellets are dissolved safely in the water.*

The author has now given us two explanations. The first is why potassium chloride is very useful as a poison in this case. The second is how the poison is going to be administered to the mussels. The structure of the argument, however, has not progressed.

There is one more paragraph.

> *By being both effective and safe, this method seems to have all that is required to attack the problem of zebra mussels. It is to be hoped that Dr Aldridge's 'biobullets' will soon be shooting their way towards them.*

The argument has now been picked up again, with a further reason and a final conclusion.

> *R(5): By being both effective and safe, (the potassium chloride) method seems to have all that is required to attack the problem of zebra mussels.*

C: It is to be hoped that Dr Aldridge's 'biobullets' will soon be shooting their way towards them.

Let's now put the structure of the argument together.

R(1): Zebra mussels eat the plankton that other animals need, effectively starving juvenile fish to death.

R(2): They also do millions of dollars-worth of damage by blocking water-intake pipes of drinking-water facilities, power-station water pipes, and those of other industrial facilities.

IC(1): The zebra mussel is now a major problem for both other wildlife and for the economy.

R(3): Zebra mussels can present a health hazard by increasing human exposure to organic pollutants such as PCBs and PAHs.

R(4): The mussels can provide a different sort of health hazard on bathing beaches in that bathers can cut their feet on the sharp edges of their shells.

IC(2) Solving the problem is an urgent need.

R(5): By being both effective and safe, (the potassium chloride) method seems to have all that is required to attack the problem of zebra mussels.

C: It is to be hoped that Dr Aldridge's 'biobullets' will soon be shooting their way towards (the zebra mussels).

Diagrammatically, we can represent this as follows.

R1 + R2

↓

IC1 + R3 + R4

↓

IC2 + R5

↓

C

By the end, we can see that, apart from the bare bones of the structure of the argument, other things are going on too. We have found explanations and examples.

ACTIVITY 2: COMMENTARY

You will have seen that these arguments have more than the structure that you are looking for. Much of the content in some of the arguments will be 'scene-setting' or providing evidence to support a particular reason. Your task, of course, was to cut through all this and to find the structure of the argument.

(1) This has the following structure.

(Either) A or B is true.
B is true.
So A is not true.

In this example, A is 'Japan intends … in the world.' B is Japan is 'spending … of the world.'

It is an example of a deductively valid argument, with the form of a disjunctive syllogism.

(2) This has the following structure.

If A is true, then B is true.
B is not true.
So A is not true.

You will have had to wait until the last three sentences to find the argument structure. What comes before is 'scene-setting' including suggested explanations for the problem of the unexpectedly low figure for the UK population from the 2001 Census.

In this example, A is 'estimate was too high'. B is 'the census figure was accurate'. Not-B (B is not true) is 'the census figures can't have been right'. Not-A (A is not true) is 'It must be that the prediction of the size of the UK population is the reliable figure'.

This is an example of 'denying the consequent' (*modus tollens*). It is therefore a deductively valid argument.

(3) This has the following structure.

(Either) A or B is true.
B is not true.
So A is true.

In this example, A is 'people … think that the poor should work harder to close the gap'. B is people 'think that the wages of poorer people should be raised …'

It is an example of a deductively valid argument, with the form of a disjunctive syllogism.

(4) This does not have a structure that fits with any of the deductively valid forms.

If we were to try to reduce it to a form that looks like any of them, we would have to do the following.

If (A) we are looking at ways of improving the diet of the UK population, (then) (B) we need to discourage people from eating so much chocolate and encourage them to eat far more vegetables. If (C) such a policy worked, (then) (D) we would see considerable benefits to health. Therefore (E) we should have such a policy.

It might have something of the look of a chain argument, but the statements are not sufficiently equivalent to be able to put it into this form. It is not an example of a deductively valid argument.

(5) This argument, however, does have the form of a chain argument.

If A, then B
If B, then C
So, if A, then C

The statements are sufficiently equivalent in this example.

A = 'the amount of savings is a measure of people's financial health'/'the amount of savings is a guide to people's financial well-being'

B = 'at least 50 per cent of the population is suffering financial ill-health'/'this percentage has these financial problems'

C = 'we need to encourage people … to save'

Because this argument is in the form of a chain argument (a hypothetical syllogism), it is deductively valid.

(6) This argument has the following structure.

If A, then B
Not-B (B is not true.)
Therefore not-A (A is not true.)

In this argument, A is '"alternative" medicine is more effective than conventional medicine at treating many disorders'. B is 'those who practise it … true'.

This is a deductively valid argument in the form of 'denying the consequent' (*modus tollens*).

(7) This argument starts by looking as if it is going to give us a chain argument. But it omits a necessary move that would fit this type of structure. Its form is as follows.

If A then B
If B, then C
Therefore C

In this argument, A is '"alternative" medicine works. B is 'it would save the NHS a lot of money'. C is 'we should welcome such medicine'.

It can be seen that this is not a deductively valid argument. The author moves from hypothetical reasoning to a conclusion that is not hypothetical. In this way, it is a flawed argument, in that the reasoning does not allow for a conclusion that is anything but hypothetical. If the conclusion had been 'if "alternative" medicine works, then we should welcome it', the argument would be valid.

(8) This argument has the following form.

If A, then B
A (is true)
Therefore B (is true)

In this argument, A is fatal road accidents for all road users other than motorcyclists. B is 'we could claim that various road safety programmes had been at least partly successful'.

It can be seen that this is a deductively valid argument. It has the form of implication (*modus ponens*).

ACTIVITY 3: COMMENTARY

The passage gives us information on the way in which women in the US were less likely in 2000 to keep their own surnames on marriage than they were in 1990. A possible explanation is given, which is that marriage is now seen as conferring a desired status upon women. In consequence, changing their surname is symbolic of this status. Though information on women in the UK is not available, the suggestion is that giving up their own surname on marriage has not been a problem for them because they see themselves as equal to their husbands.

We can see then that the information in the passage indicates that, though US and UK women approach this surname issue from different directions, the outcome is in each case one of symbolic significance. For women in the US there is the symbolic significance of the name showing a change of status. For women in the UK, giving up their name on marriage can be seen as a symbol of their perception of being equal to their husbands. This symbolism is contrasted with that of independence. In both cases, then, the choice of surname has symbolic significance (albeit different). **The correct answer is therefore (D).**

(A) is not correct. There are two problems with it. The first is that we do not have the information in the passage to enable us to infer that there is a difference between the US and the UK. The second is that there is a confusion here between the status of marriage and 'a higher status'. The latter suggests something like higher socio-economic status. There is no information in the passage on this.

(B) is not correct. The passage provides information on how women in the US are seeing marriage. But we can't see this as equivalent to the information on how women in the UK see it. If anything, the information in the passage goes the other way, with US women seeing marriage as conferring a status and UK women seeing marriage as a union of equals.

(C) is not correct. The passage doesn't give us information on women in the UK who keep their own surname on marriage, so we can't draw any inference on the reasons they have for doing so.

ACTIVITY 4: COMMENTARY

The main conclusion is 'This predicted massive growth is to be regretted.'

What other conclusions could the author have drawn? If you have suggestions other than those in the following list, this goes to demonstrate what's going on in an inductive argument. In that the conclusions are no more than probable, more than one conclusion is possible.

- People should not waste their money on organic food.

- The Soil Association should tell the truth about organic food.

- If people knew the truth about organic food, they wouldn't buy it.

- The predicted increase in the sales of organic food cannot be justified in terms of the quality of the food.

- People who buy organic food must be unaware of the evidence on it.

- People should buy food that is not organic.

REFERENCES

(1) For a very good example of the misuse of the term, see Anne Thomson's 'Critical Reasoning', Routledge, 2002, p.24 (NB: it is not Anne Thomson who gets it wrong, but Mark Lawson in *The Independent*, whom she quotes.)

(2) Much of the statistical information used in these arguments comes from Simon Briscoe, *Britain in Numbers*, Politico's Publishing, 2005

7

THE SIGNIFICANCE, PRESENTATION AND SELECTION OF INFORMATION

In Chapter 4 of *Critical Thinking for AS Level* we looked in detail at how evidence used in arguments can appear in many different ways (such as percentages, rates, raw numbers, and so on). We also looked at how we can assess the significance of evidence that's presented in arguments, by asking questions such as 'can we interpret this evidence in other ways?' and 'what happens when we look at a different time-scale?'

In this chapter, we're going to look further at the subject of evidence.

SIGNIFICANCE OF INFORMATION

You will already have learned that, in an argument, evidence is given significance by the author. At an important level, we can say that information is neutral. For example, the information that 'Antarctic air is warming faster than in the rest of the world' can be seen as simply information, just like 'London is the capital of the UK'. At another level, of course, this information can be seen as having significance. But this is where things start to get complicated. What is the significance? With regard to the information on the warming of the Antarctic air, the following have been suggested.

- Global warming is happening at different rates in different parts of the world.

- Existing climate models (which hadn't predicted this Antarctic effect) are wrong.

- Global warming could be more serious than expected, given that previous measurements of Antarctic temperature showed either no increase in temperature or even cooling.

This move from evidence to meaning or significance is very important to examine in Critical Thinking. In many ways, it is at the heart of what we do in this subject. The process can be shown in a simple way.

Fact → Explanation → Significance → Argument

This can be illustrated as follows.

> **Fact**: *the percentage of Dutch people who smoke is higher than that of any other country in the developed world. (About one-third of the adult population smokes.)*

> **Explanation**: *it could be that the Dutch history of tolerance (going back many hundreds of years) has worked against campaigns to require people to stop smoking.*

> **Significance**: *attempts to get Dutch people to stop smoking have to be more focused on persuasion (by, for example, showing them that about quarter of all deaths in Holland before the age of 70 are attributable to smoking).*

> **Argument**: *Smoking rates in Holland are the highest in the developed world. The decline in smoking in other countries (such as the UK) has been brought about by a combination of restriction and persuasion. The Dutch have a long history of tolerance, going back at least as far as the sixteenth century. Therefore attempts to reduce the level of smoking in Holland should be based not on restriction but on persuasion through health education programmes that show the health risks associated with smoking.*

What we have seen is the familiar move from evidence to argument. If we are going to respond to the argument, we could respond at any of the stages from explanation onwards. We could, for example, come up with a different explanation.

> **Explanation**: *Immigrant groups in Holland include those with very high smoking rates. For example, 63 per cent of Turkish immigrants smoke as do 54 per cent of Surinamese immigrants. Given the fact that immigrant populations are rising in Holland, we could therefore expect the smoking rates in Holland to remain high.*

This would lead us to a different significance.

> **Significance**: *part of any programme to reduce smoking amongst the Dutch population must focus on the growing immigrant communities. Without such programmes, the rate of smoking will probably remain high.*

And thus to a different argument.

Argument: Smoking rates in Holland are the highest in the developed world. The decline in smoking in other countries (such as the UK) has been brought about by a combination of restriction and persuasion. Since immigrant groups in Holland have very high rates of smoking, the Dutch government needs to develop strategies which will reduce these rates. Without such strategies, we can expect that smoking will remain a major cause of death in Holland.

In the above we have seen how one piece of evidence is used to produce two different arguments. It is this process of investing evidence with significance via explanation that enables an author to do this. It is also the route into an evaluation of arguments based on evidence.

Look at the following facts. What might be their significance?

- More houses in China have a DVD player than running hot and cold water.

- More Ethiopian doctors are practising in Chicago than in Ethiopia.

ACTIVITY 1

Read the following argument and then answer the question.

In twenty years time, women will own 60 per cent of all the personal wealth in Britain. This will be a sharp increase from the 48 per cent that they presently own. The picture is highlighted by looking at the number of millionaires in the country. Already there are 10,000 more under-45-year-old millionaires who are female than male. These figures on personal wealth need to seen in the light of a number of factors that show relevant differences between men and women. There is clear evidence that females are noticeably out-performing males in school exams. In addition, if we look at both further and higher education, we find that more women than men go on to these. This enables them to get promotion to highly-skilled jobs within companies and organisations. What is also significant is that women start climbing the property ladder much earlier than men. 63 per cent of 20-24 year-old women live away from their parents. If we look at the figure for men, it is only 44 per cent. It is clear then that women are going to be increasingly financially more successful than men. [1]

Which one of the following does the author do in looking at the predicted increase of women's share of personal wealth in the next twenty years?

(A) They generalise from all under-45 year-old female millionaires to all millionaires.

(B) They use hypothetical evidence to show why women get promoted and own property.

(C) They show that changes in the behaviour of females have caused changes in the behaviour of males.

(D) They seek to show a causal relationship between changes in personal wealth owned by males and evidence on them in relation to females.

What we often find is that in looking for how an author gives significance to evidence, we are looking for assumptions that the author must make. In other words, the author will assume that the evidence has a particular meaning. The next activity illustrates this point.

ACTIVITY 2

Use the same argument you read for Activity 1 to answer the following question. Which one of the following does the author assume in the way in which they have used the evidence presented in the argument?

(A) Evidence on the higher numbers of women than men going on to higher education cannot be used to explain the significance of the greater percentage living away from their parents.

(B) Evidence on the ways in which males and females differ in education can be used to explain why women own 48 per cent of all personal wealth.

(C) The only explanation for higher numbers of women than men going on to higher education is the better performance of females in school exams.

(D) Going on to further and higher education is a necessary condition for being promoted to highly-skilled jobs in companies and organisations.

If we are faced with evidence, we will sometimes have to make an assumption ourselves if we are going to see the evidence as having a particular significance. Look at the evidence in the following passage.

There is evidence that shows that in sport the wearing of red gives a measurable advantage. This applies whether we are looking at sports in which individuals compete with other individuals, and in which teams play against other teams. Examples of the first include the 2004 Olympics which showed that in sports such as boxing and wrestling up to 60 per cent of competitors who won wore red. Examples of the same effect with team sports can be found in football: the 2005

Cup Final between Arsenal and Manchester United resulted in victory for the red-wearing Arsenal. (And Liverpool won the European Cup in 2005, wearing red.)

As before, we can look for an explanation of the evidence.

Explanation: *The explanation for the advantage of wearing red in sport is probably that, in the animal kingdom, red is a sign of male dominance and strength, with fear being signalled by paleness. Red for danger leads to red for success.*

In looking for the significance of the evidence, we need to consider what we have to assume about the evidence itself.

To avoid the inference that poor sportspeople would expect to beat better ones if only they wore red, what do we have to assume about the evidence presented in the passage? Do any of the following have to be assumed?

(A)   The evidence looked at sportspeople who, apart from the wearing of red, were largely evenly-matched in skills and any other relevant qualities.

(B)   The evidence on the advantage of wearing red means that there are no advantages in wearing any other colours.

(C)   Sportspeople choose to wear red in order to give them an advantage over other individuals or teams.

(D)   The evidence on the advantages of wearing red applies to areas of human life apart from sport.

(A) must be assumed. The evidence has significance only if other factors which might explain advantage in sport have been taken into account. Thus if we were to use this evidence in an argument, we would need to assume that the explanation that red-wearing sportspeople have other advantages cannot be used.

(B) does not have to be assumed. This is too strong an assumption for the evidence to have to have. There might well be advantages in sportspeople wearing other colours. At the very least, though red might be the best colour, it might well be that the wearing of (say) blue has an advantage over the wearing of yellow (say). (Think of Chelsea football club.)

(C) does not have to be assumed. For the evidence to be significant, we do not have to assume that red is used to give an advantage. The evidence stands even if no sportsperson has ever seen the evidence, in that the red factor will operate anyway.

(D) does not have to be assumed. Though the explanation is likely to lead us to believe that the wearing of red does apply in contexts other than sport, we do not have to assume this in drawing any inference about its role in sport.

So what inference could we draw from the evidence, given assumption (A) above and the explanation about red being a natural signal?

> *If a sportsperson or team is going to compete against another, then they should wear red.*

It is a simple enough inference, but it fits with both the assumption and the explanation. You will see that we have given the evidence the significance of being, in one way, a causal factor in success.

The next two activities provide further practice in showing how looking at an author's use of evidence can be linked with the finding of assumptions. In particular, we are looking at how an author has to believe something in order to give the evidence the significance that they want. This belief can be made explicit or remain implicit.

ACTIVITY 3

China is planning to build the world's three highest skyscrapers. The biggest of them will be in Shanghai and, with 94 storeys, will be 260 feet higher than the Empire State Building. It will not be completed until 2012. But we should expect something to happen a little before then: a crisis in the Chinese economy. This is because of what is called the Skyscraper Index, a theory that predicts that the construction of very tall buildings precedes an economic crisis. There are many examples. The Chrysler Building was, at its completion in 1930, the world's tallest building. Seven months before, we saw the Wall Street Crash. The Petronas Tower in Malaysia was completed in 1997 just after the economic crisis that affected that part of the world. There are many more examples from history, from the Ancient Egyptians to Hitler. The Chinese would therefore be well-advised to scrap their plans for the three skyscrapers. There's trouble ahead if they don't. [2]

Which one of the following is an assumption of the above argument?
(A) Building very tall buildings is too expensive for most countries.
(B) The Chinese economy is at present expanding.
(C) The Chinese Government is unaware of the Skyscraper Index.
(D) There are no counter-examples that conflict with the Skyscraper Index.

ACTIVITY 4

A small mutation in a gene has been shown to affect how much sleep is needed. The mutation, called Shaker, was discovered in experiments with fruit flies. Those flies that had it could manage perfectly well on only a third of the amount of sleep that other fruit flies had. But the Shaker flies did not perform less well on any of the tests for mental alertness. The key factor appears to be the control by the Shaker gene of potassium to cells, which affects their electrical activity (and thus the need for sleep). The possible applications of this research are important for the development of drugs for people with sleep disorders. There are those who suffer from insomnia (who cannot sleep enough) and those who suffer from conditions such as narcolepsy (which causes people to keep falling asleep). Though the fruit flies with Shaker were mentally alert after their limited sleep, there is a downside to being able to cope with less sleep. They didn't live as long as the others. Therefore, we should be careful about developing drugs based on this research.

Which one of the following is NOT assumed in the above argument?

(A) Genetic information about fruit flies is relevant to humans.

(B) Drugs to affect the control of potassium to cells can have the same effect on sleep needs as the Shaker mutation.

(C) Drugs that affect the control of potassium to cells could be adapted to solve the problem of lower life expectancy that accompanies the Shaker mutation.

(D) Tests of mental awareness that are used with fruit flies are adequate guides to the effects of the Shaker mutation in people.

PRESENTATION OF INFORMATION

Evidence can be presented in many ways. The most common ones are the ones that we are used to working with: text and numbers. But there are others. Information can be presented, for example, in diagrams and in graphs.

INFORMATION GIVEN IN DIAGRAMS

In Chapter 6 we looked at various types of syllogistic reasoning. Given the tight structure of such reasoning, it is perhaps not surprising that we can represent these syllogisms in diagrammatic form.

One very early way of doing this is to use what are called Euler diagrams, named after their inventor Leonhard Euler (1707-1783). His diagrams can be used to represent each of the following four statements.

- All A are B.

- No A is B.

- Some A is B.

- Some A is not B.

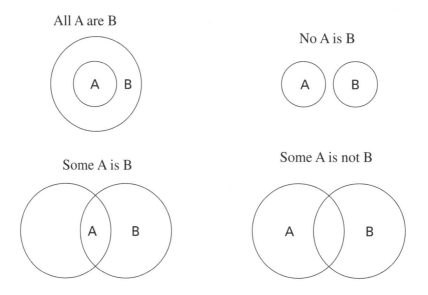

Using this method, we can represent the syllogism 'All A are B. All C are A. Therefore all C are B'.

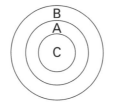

A development of the Euler diagrams is the use of Venn diagrams, named after their inventor John Venn (1834-1923). Venn argued that his diagrams gave the opportunity to express more information. Specifically, they include shading in the circles. Venn used shading to show the absence of something. Once we have understood this idea of 'shading out' rather than 'shading in', the method is a useful progression beyond the Euler diagrams. The following Venn diagrams illustrate how they can be used to give information in a non-verbal way.

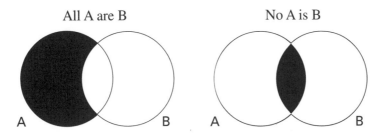

Thus both Euler and Venn diagrams can be used to represent information and the relationships between parts of it.

Other types of diagram can represent a scale. In Chapter 2, we looked at the construction of a continuum. You will remember that this represents a scale on which we can place various options. Showing it diagrammatically highlights the progression from one end of the continuum to another. Activity 5 shows information represented diagrammatically, with questions based on it. The Activity is given as two separate parts in that, though they both use similar information, the questions are different. What we are looking at is the question of how can we best explain the information that is presented in this case diagrammatically?

ACTIVITY 5(A)

Intelligence (as measured by IQ scores)
low ——————— A —————B ——————— high

Life expectancy
short ——————— A ——————— B ——————— long

The above information shows that there is a correlation between intelligence and life expectancy. To illustrate this, the positions of two people, A and B, are shown with regard to their intelligence and life expectancy.

Which one of the following is the least useful as an explanation of this correlation?

(A) The longer the life-expectancy, the more likely it is that someone applied their intelligence to do well in education.

(B) Children with low birthweight have a greater tendency to have low IQ scores and to develop heart disease and diabetes.

(C) People with high intelligence might choose a healthier lifestyle than those with lower intelligence (by, for example, not smoking and eating healthy food).

(D) People with high IQs might be able to process information more effectively, such that they can work out factors such as risk and benefits, all of which could improve their health.

ACTIVITY 5(B)

Intelligence (as measured by IQ scores)

low ——————— A ——————— B ——————— high

Life expectancy

short ——————— A ——————— B ——————— long

Reaction times

slow ——————— A ——————— B ——————— fast

The above now shows that the speed of reaction times is also correlated with intelligence and life-expectancy. A possible explanation is that low IQs and slow reaction times are early indicators of mental decline, which in turn could be leading to physical decline with a greater chance of illness.

Which one of the following could be used to provide a different explanation to the one suggested above?

(A) The speed of reaction times is a stronger prediction of life-expectancy than IQ scores.

(B) Reaction times get slower as people age, even though their IQ scores might not decline.

(C) Intelligent people's fast reaction times gives them a lower risk of being in an accident than others.

(D) 11-year-olds are too young to show any signs of mental decline, but their IQ scores show a strong correlation with life-expectancy.

INFORMATION SHOWN IN GRAPHS

Information is often provided in graphical forms. This is simple enough to understand, although clearly there might be problems of interpretation if different graphs are used together to draw inferences. Such problems could include the use of different time-scales in separate graphs and also different units of measurement involved. For example, one graph showing alcohol consumption by males aged 25-34 could show number of litres of beer consumed and another could show litres of wine consumed by the same group. We might expect that the number of litres of beer consumed would be higher, simply because of the point that people who drink beer tend to drink it in larger volumes than the people who drink wine. The information couldn't necessarily enable us to draw the inference that beer was a more popular drink than wine.

If we look at the next three graphs, they give us information on three things between the years 1995-2005. They are not based on actual figures but we will look at them simply as an exercise on inference. The first shows an obvious decline in play areas over this period; the second shows an obvious increase in childhood obesity over the same; the third shows an obvious increase in the number of fast-food outlets during these years.

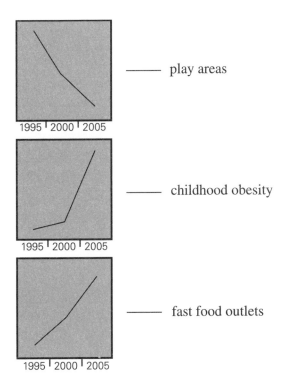

———— play areas

———— childhood obesity

———— fast food outlets

Could we draw any inferences from these three graphs taken together? In particular, could we draw any causal inferences from them? A recent report by the organisation CABE has claimed that 'our open spaces are a powerful weapon in the fight against obesity and ill-health.'[3] The same report recommends an expansion of public space for us all to use for various recreational purposes. So would this evidence be able to support the claim by CABE?

The first two graphs would be relevant in showing a correlation between the decline in play areas and the growth of childhood obesity. If one wanted to support CABE's claim, then these first two graphs would be relevant to it. But we have to be careful. CABE is claiming that we can use open spaces to reduce obesity. The claim isn't that a decline in these spaces has in part led to an increase in obesity.

What about the third graph? This shows an increase in fast-food outlets which has an inverse correlation with the decline in play areas. Would we expect to see anything beyond this inverse correlation? Could we find anything causal here? We could be creative and say that, as fast-food outlets have increased, so childhood obesity has gone up, so there has been a reduction in play areas because lots of obese children aren't going to want to play outside. We could put it round a different way. As the number of play areas has gone down, the more it is that children are taken to fast-food outlets by their parents for special treats (rather than a game of rounders in the park), thus leading via both routes (less exercise, more unhealthy food) to an increase in childhood obesity.

In the end, of course, though we can suggest inferences that show a causal relationship between the information in the three graphs, we cannot demonstrate any causal relationship between the three. The fact that the data support such a causal relationship (and are relevant to it) does not mean that we can avoid the accusation of an inappropriate *post hoc* inference.

The next activity asks you to look at graphs to see how they correspond to information given in words and numbers.

ACTIVITY 6

In this activity, we are looking at how information in graphs can correspond with information given in other ways.
In this example, we are considering what happened to both membership and income of a new organisation during its first year of existence. This is a fictional example.

Action Against Animal Cruelty (preferring to be known as *3xA+C*) was set up in January 2005 in order to focus pressure on the Government in order to get it to stop allowing medical experimentation on animals, especially primates. It had a particularly successful start to its campaign after it had shown secret footage of monkeys undergoing very painful procedures in a UK laboratory.

3xA+C encouraged people to join by offering annual membership of only £10 during the first six months of its existence. Those who joined in the next three months were able to have annual membership for £15; those who joined in the next three months after that were asked to pay £20.

Membership during the first six months went from zero to 150,000. During the next three months, it increased by 35,000; during the final three months it went up by 18,000.

After their first year, the leaders of *3xA+C* have decided to review their membership fees and have asked to be given graphs showing details of membership and income during the year. They have asked for the latter to show cumulative income, that is how much their income has risen over the year. Which two graphs should they be given?

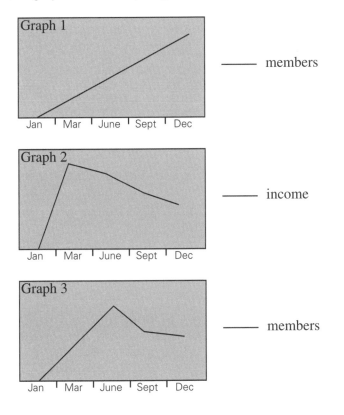

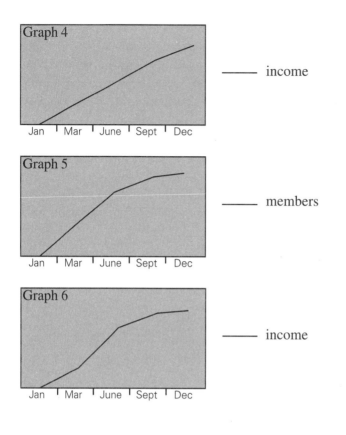

SELECTION OF INFORMATION

Both in putting together an argument and in evaluating an existing one, we often need to look for information that is relevant. In doing so, we can be faced with a range of information some of which will be relevant, some less so, and some irrelevant. We need to select from this information.

In the following example, we are given some information on plastic bottles and steel cans.[4]

Plastic bottles

- *£1.7 billion spent on these each year in the UK.*

- *The market for bottled water is predicted to increase by 9 per cent a year between 2005-2010.*

- *Sales of bottled water rose by 50 per cent between 2000-2005.*

- *Plastic bottles create 500,000 tonnes of rubbish which is not bio-degradable every year in the UK.*

- *Each plastic bottle takes 450 years to break down if put into a landfill site.*

- *Most water bottles are made from PET, which is derived from crude-oil.*

Steel cans

- *13 billion cans are used in the UK every year.*

- *About 2.5 billion of them are recycled every year.*

- *Using scrap steel can save can save 70 per cent of the energy required to make cans from iron ore.*

Does the evidence enable us to produce an argument showing the advantages of recycling?

It gives an advantage with regard to steel cans (the saving of energy), but does it with plastic bottles? It gives two pieces of evidence that show a problem with not recycling the bottles (the plastic is not bio-degradable – except after 450 years – and the very large amount of waste bottles). However, this evidence on bottles does not strictly enable us to argue that we should recycle them. It is perhaps more relevant to an argument that we shouldn't use these bottles at all.

What further evidence do we need to produce an argument in favour of recycling?

With regard to both steel cans and plastic bottles, we would need to know about the costs of recycling. We have some relevant information on how recycling steel cans saves energy, but we need to know about transport and other costs (including environmental costs) that arise from the process of recycling.

With regard to plastic bottles, we need to know much more. What percentage of bottles are actually recycled, and with what costs? Here are the answers to those questions.

- *Only 8 per cent of plastic bottles in the UK are recycled each year (out of an estimated total of 9.2 billion).*

- *4000 tonnes of plastic bottles were recycled in 2005 by being sent to China for processing.*

- *Most of the bottles sent to China are incinerated.*

- *Since China is about 13,000 kilometres away from the UK, transporting the bottles there produces about 500,000 kilograms of CO_2 emissions.*

Does this evidence support the case for recycling plastic bottles?
Should we aim to increase the figure from 8 per cent?

In many ways, the answer is 'no' since the environmental costs appear to be much too high.

So what argument does this evidence support? It would fit very well with an argument against the use of plastic bottles in the first place. In which case, should we be looking for evidence in favour of using an alternative to these bottles, with the obvious candidate being glass? Here is some evidence you might need for such an argument.

- *Recycled glass needs only 75 per cent of the energy used in making glass in the first place.*

- *For every tonne of recycled glass, 112 tonnes of raw materials are saved.*

- *Glass can be recycled into a material to make roads. About 14 million bottles were used in the building of the M6 motorway.*

- *34 per cent of glass used for containers in this country is recycled.*

The first three pieces of evidence are certainly relevant to an argument for recycling of glass. They are therefore also relevant to an argument that we should put our water into glass rather than plastic bottles. The fourth piece of evidence is, in a way, neutral. What is its significance? If we learn that Finland recycles 90 per cent of its glass, its significance could be that we should increase our recycling rate for glass (given that another country has shown it can be done).

If we take all of the evidence that we have looked at, was any of it irrelevant to any of the arguments that we have been considering?

The very first piece of evidence, that of the amount spent on plastic bottles in the UK, is not obviously relevant. It gives an idea of the scale of the demand, but does not enable us to conclude anything about recycling. The second piece of evidence on the projected increase in the market for bottled water is relevant if two suppositions are added to it. The first is that the bottled water will continue to be supplied in plastic bottles (which is a reasonable supposition). The second is that the status quo with regard to the recycling of plastic bottles is maintained. In other words, given the environmental problems of the present situation (most plastic bottles buried in landfill sites; most of the bottles sent for recycling are burned), the problems will increase as demand goes up. The third piece of evidence on the increase in sales between 2000-2005 has no obvious relevance to such arguments, except again to emphasise the scale of the problem.

The sixth piece of evidence on plastic bottles, that most are made from PET, needs further information if we are to use it in one of these arguments. We are told that PET is derived from crude-oil, but is this a problem in itself? The production of PET (polyethylene terephthalate, for those of you who want to know) requires 220,000 barrels of crude oil a year to cover the demand for bottles in the UK. Does this tell us more? For those of you who worry about the extraction and use of oil, presumably yes. For those of you who worry less about these things, presumably no, especially as PET bottles are responsible for only about 0.25 per cent of the world's total oil consumption.

So, next time, you buy water in a plastic bottle, consider this argument further. (And, whilst you're at it, consider the evidence of the costs of bringing that water to you. Many bottled waters travel thousands of kilometres before they reach you …)

ACTIVITY 1: COMMENTARY

This exercise shows how an author can provide a lot of evidence and, by giving the evidence an explanation and thus significance, produces an argument based on it. Crucially the author believes that this evidence can be seen in a causal way. Females performing better than males in school exams; the higher proportion of females continuing their education after school; the higher proportion of 20-24 year-old women living away from their parents: all these separate pieces of evidence are used to predict that women are going to be increasingly financially more successful than men. What the author has done is to see this evidence as having the significance of a causal relationship. It has caused and will continue to cause the decline in males' financial success. **The answer is therefore (D).**

(A) is not correct. Though the author sees the evidence on under-45 year-old female millionaires as having significance for their prediction that women will continue to be more financially successful than men, the author does not use this evidence to generalise to all millionaires. Indeed, even if over-45 year-old millionaires had a male majority, the author's argument would be unaffected. They are making a prediction based on the evidence of under-45s rather than seeing the under-45s as typical of the over-45s.

(B) is not correct. Though the author uses 'if ...' on two occasions, this is not to present hypothetical evidence. For example, it is not arguing 'if more women than men go on to further and higher education, then ...'

(C) is not correct. Though the evidence on females is used to explain why they will be more financially successful than males, it is not used to show that the behaviour of females has caused males to behave differently.

ACTIVITY 2: COMMENTARY

Two pieces of evidence which are used separately by the author could be linked in a causal way. These are the higher proportion of females going on to higher education and the higher proportion of 20-24 year-old females living away from home. It could be that (at least in part) the first explains the second. If more females than males go to college and university, then we might expect that, in consequence, more females than males will live away from their parents. Thus we can suggest a causal relationship between the two pieces of evidence. In that the author does not make this causal link (seeing the evidence as having significance separately), **the author has to assume (A).**

Though the author links the evidence on education with the prediction that women will be more financially successful than men, they do not do this explicitly with the evidence that women currently own 48 per cent of personal wealth. The author might see these in a causal way but the argument does not require that they do. The argument is centrally about why this figure of 48 per cent will increase to 60 per cent. **Thus (B) is not correct.**

(C) is not correct. The author is not committed to seeing this as the only explanation. They might want to offer a number of explanations, of which this is only one. The negative test for assumptions (see the AS book pages 57-58) will highlight this point. What would happen to the argument if the author was required to believe that 'there are other explanations for higher numbers of women than men going on to higher education beside the better performance of females in school exams'? The answer is 'nothing'. Quite simply, the author could argue in just the same way. Thus (C) is not an assumption.

(D) is not correct. The author clearly links further and higher education with promotion to highly-skilled jobs. But the author is not required to believe that education is a necessary condition of promotion. Again, the negative test will show that the author could happily accept the negative form of this statement without their argument being affected.

ACTIVITY 3: COMMENTARY

This argument is interesting in this context because it provides two different types of evidence. One is various examples of when the construction of very tall buildings preceded an economic crisis. The other is the theory based on these examples, the Skyscraper Index. The author uses the latter to draw the conclusion that 'The Chinese would therefore be well-advised to scrap their plans for the three skyscrapers.' In an important way, the evidence of the specific examples is unnecessary for the argument in that the Skyscraper Index is enough for the conclusion to be drawn. So what must the author assume about the evidence they provide?

Crucially, they have to assume (D). The evidence of the Skyscraper Index enables the author to draw a conclusion that is based on the predictive quality of the Index. However, if there are counter-examples that show that the Index is no more than (at best) a general guide to the correlation between the building of tall buildings and economic crisis, then the author's argument is less strong. This is especially so, given the author's prediction that 'There's trouble ahead if they don't'. In this way, the author has to assume that there are no counter-examples which would reduce the predictive power of the Index.

(A) does not have to be assumed. Though the explanation of the correlation between the building of tall buildings and economic crisis might be something to do with countries over-reaching themselves, this is an unlikely explanation. The author does not have this statement as the assumed explanation for the Index, in that the argument works without it. Anyway, 'most' countries would weaken the significance of the Index. It would allow 'some' countries to be able to afford such buildings.

(B) does not have to be assumed. Though the author gives examples that show that successful (expanding) economies can suffer following the building of tall buildings, the author does not have to assume that the Chinese economy is at present expanding. It could just be doing OK, so to speak. Economies don't have to either be expanding or in crisis.

(C) does not have to be assumed. The author's use of the evidence of the Skyscraper Index does not have less significance if the Chinese Government knows about the Index. They might simply decide to ignore it. In this way, the significance of the evidence is not weakened either way.

ACTIVITY 4: COMMENTARY

This activity introduces a different type of question. It is one that has a negative in it. You will not have met such questions before at AS level. But at A2 level you can expect to find them. In one way, there's no difference between being asked 'what is assumed?' and 'what is not assumed?' In each case, you're looking at the options and making a decision. You will need to be careful, however, that you keep the negative in your thinking when making a choice. This is because you're so used to doing it the other way round that as soon as you find an assumption you're inclined to think 'there's my answer!' With this question, of course, it's the other way round.

What we are looking for is what the author does not need to assume for the evidence presented here to have the significance they intend.

(A) is in a typical category of assumptions needed when evidence is being used. This is that the evidence that has been found in one situation is applicable to another. There is often no good reason to doubt the applicability, although situations can be relevantly different. In this case, the author has to assume that the discovery of the genetic mutation called Shaker in fruit flies is relevant to humans. This is required because the author argues that 'possible applications of this research are important for the development of drugs for people with sleep disorders'.

(B) is also assumed. The author argues that the discovery of the Shaker gene and how it affects the need for sleep (by means of the control of potassium to the cells) is relevant to people with sleep disorders (as above). Specifically the author sees this research as relevant to the development of drugs for people with sleep disorders. Such drugs, the author must believe, would have to work in the same way as the Shaker gene, by controlling potassium.

(C) is the one that is not assumed. The author concludes that 'we should be careful about developing drugs' which work like the Shaker gene because of the problem of shorter life span. If these drugs could be adapted to solve this problem, then the author's conclusion cannot be drawn. In this way, the author cannot assume (C). Rather, if you apply the negative test, they must assume the opposite. (Check it to see.)

(D) is, on the other hand, assumed. This has a similar force to the assumption in (A). The author does not have to assume that the tests of mental awareness used with fruit flies are ones that would have to be used to test the effect of the Shaker mutation in humans. But they do have to assume that the tests used with fruit flies provide adequate evidence of the effects of the gene on people. Unless they do (try the negative test), the argument falls in that the author cannot apply the research to humans. This is, then, another example in which the author has to assume something about the significance of the evidence.

ACTIVITY 5(A): COMMENTARY

You will have noticed that this was another example of a negative question. We are looking for the 'least useful' explanation.

The diagram shows a straightforward correlation between intelligence and life-expectancy. No argument is presented, so no explanation is given of the evidence. The task was therefore unusual in that we are normally evaluating the author's explanation and judgement of the significance of the evidence.

The least useful explanation for the correlation is (A). It doesn't even provide an explanation as such. It suggests that long life-expectancy is correlated with success in education, but doesn't show why intelligence and life-expectancy are themselves correlated.

(B) provides an explanation for the correlation. It suggests that there is a third factor ('low birthweight') which explains the correlation. Low birthweight in this way is correlated with lower intelligence and lower life expectancy.

(C) provides a possible explanation for the correlation. If people with high intelligence have a healthier lifestyle, then we would expect them to have a longer life expectancy.

(D) also provides a possible explanation for the correlation. This time it is the more effective processing of information which enables higher intelligence people to make better judgements of risk and benefits. Of course, we have to assume that, having worked out risk and benefits, they act upon their judgements. Without this assumption, the explanation does not work.

ACTIVITY 5(B): COMMENTARY

The information in the diagram is now expanded to show a third variable that correlates with the other two. This time we are given an explanation for the evidence. Our task was to find a different one.

(A) is not correct. The three variables of intelligence, life expectancy, and reaction times are shown to correlate equally with each other. (A) suggests that this is not the case.

(B) is not correct. This does not explain the correlation between fast reaction times and long life expectancy. In fact, it suggests that a long life would be correlated with slow reaction times which is the opposite of what the evidence suggests.

(C) does provide a different explanation. This brings together all three of the variables and shows how they could be correlated. As a result of faster reaction times, intelligent people will have fewer accidents, resulting in a higher life expectancy.

(D) is not correct. This makes no reference to the speed of reaction times. In addition, it provides no explanation of any sort.

ACTIVTY 6: COMMENTARY

The information we are given has to correspond to two of the graphs, one showing membership and the other showing income.

If we look at membership first, we need to find a graph which shows a rapid increase in membership from January, with membership continuing to increase but at a slower rate between June and September, and then at an even slower rate until the end of December. Graph 5 shows this trend. Graph 1 showed a consistent increase in the rate of growth which does not therefore fit the figures. Graph 3 shows a change in the rate of growth but does not show that, though the rate slows, membership continues to increase.

If we look at income, we are looking for the cumulative increase in income over the year. In other words, how does the total increase over the year? Graph 4 shows this. It shows that income continues to grow over the year, although not at the rate of the first six months. The first six months produced £1,500,000; the next three months produced an additional £525,000; the next three months added a further £360,000. Thus, though the amount added declined, the overall total continued to increase.

Graph 2 fails to show the cumulative increase in income. It shows income as declining after June which does not take account of the continuing growth of income. Graph 6 shows income as reaching a plateau at September which again does not take account of a continuing increase in income after that date.

REFERENCES

(1) Based on information reported in *Metro*, 22 April 2005

(2) Based on information in Paul Johnson, 'Last one to leave the skyscraper, please turn out the lights', *The Spectator*, 14 May 2005

(3) The Value of Public Space,' Commission for Architecture and the Built Environment (CABE), 2004

(4) Much of this information comes from *The Times*, 18 February 2006

8

GETTING FURTHER INSIDE ARGUMENTS

Arguments await our attention to be understood, evaluated, and responded to. By now you can do all of these things. But we'll do some more work so that you can do them even better.

CONSISTENCY AND INCONSISTENCY

Looking for **consistency** in an argument is a very important task in Critical Thinking. We react against arguments that take an inconsistent line, unless the reasons for taking such a line make clear how it can be justified. These reasons would be likely to show that what appears as inconsistency is only apparent rather than real. There are differences between situations that, for example, make something acceptable in one but not the other.

Inconsistency is also relevant when assessing an author's use of evidence. If evidence that is used points an argument in different directions, then an author who ignores this problem is open to the charge of inconsistency. For example, if we have an argument that medical experiments on animals are always justified by the fact that drugs that have been tested on animals have resulted in huge improvements in medical care, then the author would be risking inconsistency if they acknowledged that some drugs have had the opposite effect. What normally happens, of course, is that an author doesn't acknowledge the existence of inconsistent evidence. This is the practice of 'cherry picking' by which an author chooses only that evidence that supports their position. If they do show the inconsistent evidence, they will normally seek to show why the evidence, though inconsistent, can be shown not to be typical or reliable or not having the significance that has been given it (by giving a different explanation for it).

The next activity focuses on finding out how the author has argued, and then asks you to find arguments that do the same (in order to find one that doesn't). It links with consistency by asking you to look for a principle that the author of the first argument has used, and then looking for the application of this principle in other arguments.

ACTIVITY 1

Students are more likely to cheat in tests if they feel that they have not been taught well. Students appear to have a clear sense of what they expect from their teachers: they expect to be taught sufficiently well in order to be able to succeed. If this has not happened, then students justify their cheating by seeing it as a way of making things fairer for themselves. It is obvious then that we should not condemn such students. After all, they are doing no more than trying to make life more socially just, a goal that we all aspire to. [1]

Which one of the following does NOT use the same justification for action as the above argument?

(A) If a swimming club has no adequate training facilities, it is entitled to receive more support from the Amateur Swimming Association than those clubs whose training facilities are adequate.

(B) Very small countries win very few, if any, Olympic medals. If their athletes use performance-enhancing drugs, it is difficult to see why they should be punished as severely as athletes from countries that are very successful in the Olympics.

(C) If a Formula One racing car has been designed such that it is faster than any others, the car's driver cannot be described as cheating if he uses that advantage to win the race.

(D) If a football club is owned by a billionaire, then no other clubs will be able to out-bid it when it comes to buying players. Since we can't stop billionaires buying football cubs, we should have a handicap system in operation by which poorer clubs are given extra points for winning matches.

This activity gave you practice in seeing what is going in an argument and applying this to a different context. In terms of looking at consistency, it could be that, if you've agreed with the first argument, you would have to justify your inconsistency in rejecting those that used the same method.

In the argument on students cheating in tests, the author argues that this is acceptable because it is done in order to achieve fairness. This does not mean that the author has to be consistent by approving of students cheating in all situations. Well-taught students cannot use the defence of compensating for the quality of their teaching.

Questions that look at inconsistency can be of the familiar 'which of the following, if true, would most weaken the argument?' that you have met before. They can also explicitly ask for 'which of the following is inconsistent with the argument?' We'll meet other questions on inconsistency when we look at longer passages in the next chapter.

ACTIVITY 2

A study in the US has shown that people who are only moderately overweight have a lower risk of death than those who are at what is supposedly their ideal weight. It is only the grossly obese who have a greatly increased risk. Indeed, if we look at the other end of the scale, though it might be seen as very desirable to be very skinny (like, for example, Kate Moss), evidence shows that such skinny people have a higher risk of death than those who are heavier. Such evidence provides a very welcome counter-balance to the constant pressure that is put upon us to keep our weight down. Being moderately overweight should no longer be seen as a problem. Indeed, gyms and slimming organisations should be attacked for peddling mischief and for making people feel unnecessarily guilty and inadequate. Goodbye lycra; hello doughnut.

Which one of the following would **most weaken** the above argument?
(A) The risks of being overweight include disease and disability as well as death.
(B) Being grossly obese has a higher risk of death than being very underweight.
(C) The risks associated with being overweight have been reduced as a result of the availability of drugs that can control blood pressure and cholesterol levels.
(D) Obesity is included in the seven biggest killers in the US, after tobacco, alcohol, germs, toxins and pollutants, cars, and guns.

ACTIVITY 3

Though some newspapers make much of the issue of asylum applications, the number of such applications has declined sharply as most of them are refused. Anyway, we should look at the issue of migration in a much wider perspective. Migration affects the UK in both directions. People emigrate to countries such as New Zealand, and people come into the UK from abroad. If we take both figures together, we have a figure for net migration. For many years, this has remained at around +150,000. Many employers (such as farmers, restaurant-owners, and working mothers) depend on people from poor countries to provide low-wage labour. Skilled immigrants are needed by banks and hospitals. Even home-owners benefit, especially in London, by foreign workers keeping property prices up. There is also the benefit that, as our population gets older, it needs younger workers (which immigrants are) to pay for the pensions of the old and to care for them as they become more dependent. There is nothing but benefits from immigration. It is obvious then that we should ensure that immigration is not jeopardised by some misguided newspapers.

Which one of the following is **inconsistent** with the author's argument?
(A) Immigration can solve many current economic problems facing the UK.
(B) The level of immigration into the UK needs to increase over the next few years.
(C) Emigration from the UK needs to be at a lower level than immigration into the country.
(D) Immigration into the UK can create resentment amongst some unskilled workers, by keeping wages low.

When we are looking for consistency, one thing we can do is to see if the reasons used in an argument are consistent with each other. The argument in Activity 3 used the following reasons to draw its intermediate conclusion.

R(1): Many employers (such as farmers, restaurant-owners, and working mothers) depend on people from poor countries to provide low-wage labour.

R(2): Skilled immigrants are needed by banks and hospitals.

R(3): Even home-owners benefit, especially in London, by foreign workers keeping property prices up.

R(4): There is also the benefit that, as our population gets older, it needs younger workers (which immigrants are) to pay for the pensions of the old and to care for them as they become more dependent.

IC: There is nothing but benefits from immigration.

The reasons are consistent both with each other and with the intermediate conclusion. By being consistent, they strengthen the argument. We can recognise the value of consistency when we look at questions in which we are asked to find evidence which would strengthen an argument. Such evidence could provide an additional reason to support the conclusion or provide evidence that supports an existing reason.

ACTIVITY 4

The number of attacks by great white sharks on people has been increasing recently because of the boom in what's called 'shark-cage-diving'. Thousands of tourists each year, in Australia and South Africa, are attracted to this 'sport', in which you are placed in a cage which is lowered into the water. Sharks are attracted to the location by putting fish blood and guts into the water. When the shark arrives, its snout is often prodded by people on the boat, just so that it will open its mouth to show its terrifying teeth. This is similar to what used to be done with lions and leopards and this is fortunately no longer permitted. In addition, putting humans and sharks together is unnatural. Both humans and sharks have traditionally avoided each other, for good reasons. Now, we are encouraging a familiarity between the two, such that the sharks will associate humans with food. Recognising this problem, California has banned shark-cage-diving. It is time that their lead was followed by Australia and South Africa, and a ban brought in not only for the sake of swimmers and divers, but also for that of the much-maligned great white shark.

Which one of the following, if true, would **most strengthen** the above argument?

(A) In August 2004, great white sharks killed two people, one in Australia and the other in California.

(B) Great white sharks are protected in most parts of the world from any interference with their lives.

(C) The data on great white shark attacks include not only fatal attacks, but also the number of people who are injured but not killed.

(D) Many tour operators provide opportunities for tourists to swim with small reef sharks outside cages.

ACTIVITY 5

In this exercise, you are asked to identify some evidence which strengthens a particular reason that the author uses.

Increasingly we live in a society that suffers from 'infomania'. This is the problem of feeling the need to respond to e-mails and texts as soon as they arrive. It has been found that it can temporarily lower IQ by as much as ten points. The explanation for 'infomania' is that 'always-on' technology distracts people from what they should be doing. At work, people are in a constant state of readiness, waiting for the next e-mail or text to arrive. This prevents them from concentrating on what they should be doing. Quite simply, the brain finds it difficult to cope with lots of tasks going on at the same time. In that this problem reduces the efficiency of people at work, employers should take steps to stop their staff from feeling the need to respond to e-mails and texts as soon as they get them.

The following are pieces of evidence relevant to the problem of 'infomania'. Which of these would most strengthen the reason the author uses why employers should try to stop their staff responding to e-mails and texts as soon as they get them?

(A) 62 per cent of people admit that they check work e-mails and texts even when they are on holiday.

(B) The need to keep answering e-mails and texts increases the rate of stress and the number of arguments at work.

(C) Many employers give gadgets and devices to their staff so that they can keep in touch even when they are not at their place of work.

(D) One in three people in the UK believes that it is not only acceptable but also a sign of efficient working if e-mails and texts are responded to straightaway.

FURTHER ISSUES OF DEFINITION

This is just a brief return to the issue of definition. We spent some time looking at this subject in Chapter 1, but we shall spend a very little time longer on this subject. This is because definitions can play such an important part in some arguments. We therefore need to be on the look-out for them.

When an author produces or uses a definition, we need to be sure that it is being given in a neutral way. Very often this won't be the case. Jeremy Bentham made a distinction between 'eulogistic' and 'dyslogistic' ways of describing something. This distinction is between the description of something in a favourable or unfavourable way. For example, someone might commend 'the value of freedom of speech which is the basis of all other freedoms' yet at the same time condemn 'giving licence to those who wish to cause trouble by inciting others to hate other groups'. The contrast between 'freedom' and 'licence' is in many ways completely artificial: they are both the same thing.

This problem also arises in what is called the 'definist fallacy'. This involves defining a term in such a way that the definition works favourably for a particular argument. We have met an example of this when we looked at libertarianism. To define taxation as theft by the State is to provide a definition that already fits with one's argument. It could be seen in this way as part of a circular or question-begging argument. Another example of this would be when an author goes through the motions of trying to define something in order to argue that, since it is impossible to produce a definition, there is no such thing.

We are so used to hearing about 'junk food' that we don't stop to think what this is. I have just eaten a bar of chocolate, so does this mean that I've eaten junk food? The packet tells me that I've eaten 8.1 grams of protein amongst the mixture of cocoa mass, sugar, cocoa butter, and soya lecithin. So are protein and cocoa on the list of junk food? The evidence on the health value of dark chocolate is considerable, so cocoa can't be on the list of junk food. Protein is essential to our diet, so it also can't be junk food. So, how can we define it? Foods that are high in sugar? Well, that rules out fruit. Foods that are low in nutrition? Well, that rules out cucumber and lettuce. Foods like burgers? Well, that's protein gone again. No, whichever way you try to define it, junk food cannot be nailed down. So, eat what you like: junk food doesn't exist.

It is clear that the author's conclusion that 'junk food doesn't exist' is drawn only from their (deliberately) unsuccessful attempt to define it. (However, to be fair to the author, how can we define it?)

CHARITY AND OTHER PRINCIPLES

We are used to looking at arguments and finding weaknesses in them. We have also tried to find strengths in arguments, in that some arguments can have good reasons leading to conclusions that are not overdrawn.

There are two principles that have been suggested that should inform the way in which we approach arguments. The first is the **principle of charity**; the second is the **principle of humanity**. The first encourages us to look at an argument and to seek to maximise the truth or rationality in it. Rather than just be sceptical of evidence that's presented, we should approach it in a principle of charity and thus consider that it might after all be true. For example, recent research has suggested that being prayed for when we're ill might either have no effect or might even make us worse. Though evidence that being prayed for might make us more ill seems very odd (and so difficult to believe), it should be accepted as worthy of consideration. This principle of charity can be linked with the principle of humanity, with the latter stressing that, even if we can't see truth in what others are arguing, we could at least see that it might be reasonable.

Another principle is called the **principle of indifference**. This works very simply. If we have a number of positions that could each be right and we don't have enough information to know which is right, then each of them has an equal probability of being right. This principle therefore invites us not to reject a position even though we haven't got evidence to support it. Though the principle is not one that can be wholeheartedly commended in that it can lead to absurd positions, it is a useful corrective to the idea that, since there is no evidence for x, x cannot exist.

A further principle is that of the **excluded middle**. This is sometimes given as both a principle and a law. It is simple to describe. The principle or law states that there is either p or there is not-p. The middle that is excluded is that which would occupy the position between p being true or false. What sort of middle is this? There could be degrees of truth or falsehood. P could be half-true or mostly true (or mostly false). The real world could have degrees of p-ness (if you'll excuse the term). The question of global warming is a bit like this. It's normally presented as 'there is global warming' or 'there isn't global warming'. Different types of evidence seems to take us in different directions. But the excluded middle offers us 'there is global warming in certain parts of the world' or 'there is some evidence of global warming but it is not at a level which some researchers have argued'.

BEING RHETORICAL AND BEING LOGICAL

A famous distinction between what is called rhetoric and what is logic was made by the early Greek philosopher Zeno. He is quoted by the Roman writer Cicero in the following way: Zeno 'clenching his fist … said logic was like that; relaxing and extending his hand, he said eloquence was like the open palm.'[2] For 'eloquence' read 'rhetoric'. You can probably identify with the first part of this analogy. Critical Thinking has, in part, encouraged (or even required) you to think like a clenched fist. If you think back to the work we did on syllogisms, then you will see that it was clenched fist all the way with those. When we think of inductive arguments on the other hand, we can see that there is more scope for the open palm. The inclusion of scene-setting, the more extravagant flourishes of language, the scope for using analogies, and so on: all these allow for the open palm of rhetoric.

Though inductive arguments can accommodate rhetoric in this way, we have to be careful to spot when rhetoric is used instead of good reasoning. In an article by Simon Jenkins in which he argues against the banning of tobacco advertising, he points out that 'life is not perfect'.[3] He says this in a particular context: 'I find police sirens, mobile phones in restaurants and dirty streets offensive.' The point that he develops is that, just because some things are found offensive by some people, this does not mean that we should ban them (especially when smoking is a legal activity). The point about legality is a good piece of argumentation: why should we ban the advertising of an activity that is legal? But his point that 'life is not perfect' is much less successful as a piece of inductive reasoning. This is because it doesn't help the argument much. You could turn it back on Jenkins to say: 'stop moaning about the ban on tobacco advertising because life is not perfect.' In this way, we have Jenkins engaging in rhetoric, in persuasive language, in using words in a way that are not meant to be understood in a literal way.

We already know that arguments are meant to be persuasive. So how can we distinguish between those that are based on rhetoric and those that are based more on (inductive) logic? It is a huge area, and one which we do not need to delve too deeply into. The distinction itself as we have seen is a very old one. If we are looking for the most persuasive argument without regard to the standards of judgement we are used to applying in Critical Thinking, then a poor inductive argument could still be a very persuasive argument. Hitler's speeches at Nazi rallies might be poor in Critical Thinking terms but still very powerfully persuasive. By the same token, a well-argued case using relevant evidence which responds to counter-arguments in an effective way might be less persuasive than a hysterical rant. Certain ranting newspapers manage to sell a lot of copies, after all.

ACTIVITY 1: COMMENTARY

The first task was obviously to work out how the author has argued that it is obvious that we shouldn't condemn those students who feel they have been badly-taught who cheat in tests. They explain how the students see cheating as a means of restoring fairness. The author reinforces this point by arguing that 'we all aspire to' social justice, and since fairness can be seen as social justice, the conclusion is strengthened. So we are looking for an argument that does not have an appeal to fairness at its centre.

(A) does use the fairness principle. It uses the same idea of discriminating in favour of a disadvantaged group in order to bring them closer to the level of advantaged groups.

(B) does use the fairness principle. The author argues that the issue of cheating by the use of performance-enhancing drugs by athletes from very small countries should be seen as a way of these athletes trying to bring themselves closer to athletes from more successful countries. Treating these athletes more leniently can be justified in terms of fairness.

(C) does not appeal to a fairness principle. The author dismisses the idea of cheating in a situation in which a Formula One racing driver uses the superior capacity of the car to win. There is no reference to discrimination to justify positive action.

(D) does use the fairness principle. It justifies treating poorer football clubs more favourably on the basis that this would bring them up to the level of richer clubs.

ACTIVITY 2: COMMENTARY

The argument uses evidence on the death rate to show that, since moderately overweight people have a rate that is lower than people who are at their 'ideal weight' or the very underweight, 'being moderately overweight should no longer be seen as a problem.'

(A) provides evidence that the author has not considered and which is inconsistent with their conclusion. Being overweight could still be a problem if we look beyond the death rate to rates of disease and disability.

(B) provides evidence which could be consistent with the author's conclusion. The author acknowledges that the grossly obese have an increased risk of death. On the other hand, they do argue that very 'skinny people have a higher risk of death than those who are heavier', but the latter group is left undefined. At one level, then, the evidence is consistent; at another, depending on definition, it is inconsistent.

(C) provides a possible explanation of why the death rate for people who are moderately overweight has been kept down. It is in this way not inconsistent with the argument. The author could still argue that 'Being moderately overweight should not any longer be seen as a problem' in that the problems associated with the condition can be controlled by drugs.

(D) could be consistent with the argument. The author is not saying that obesity as such isn't a health problem, in that they refer to the problems of the 'grossly obese'. The evidence could also be seen as showing that obesity is much less of a problem than might have been considered, being only seventh on the list of causes of death.

(A) turns out to be the evidence that is most inconsistent with the author's argument. If it is true, then the author's argument is weakened by showing that the author cannot conclude that being moderately overweight isn't a problem.

ACTIVITY 3: COMMENTARY

The argument concludes that 'It is obvious … that we should ensure that immigration is not jeopardised by some misguided newspapers.' This conclusion is drawn on the strength of four reasons which lead to an intermediate conclusion that 'There is nothing but benefits from immigration.' If we are looking for evidence that is inconsistent with this argument, we would need evidence that shows a lack of benefit of immigration. This is a problem with the author's argument. The intermediate conclusion is so strongly worded that it invites the problem of inconsistency.

(A) is entirely consistent with the author's argument. Solving 'many economic problems facing the UK' is a further benefit to be added to the list.

(B) would be consistent with the author's argument that immigration is something that should continue.

(C) looks as if it takes a different position from that of the author. However, the author could accept (C) without its being inconsistent with their argument. This is because the author could acknowledge that there is a case for keeping emigration below the level of immigration without having to concede that there are problems with immigration. (C) has not shown something that is inconsistent with the conclusion that we should ensure that immigration is not threatened by misguided newspaper reports.

(D), however, does present a problem of inconsistency. It gives evidence of something that shows that immigration might present a problem. The author's intermediate conclusion that immigration provides only benefits comes up against a lack of a benefit. As a result, (D) is inconsistent with the argument.

ACTIVITY 4: COMMENTARY

The conclusion of this argument is that it is time that Australia and South Africa banned the practice of shark-cage-diving. If we are looking for evidence to strengthen this argument, we can see that **(B) provides some which will provide another line of argument**. (B) does this by something of an appeal to consistency. The argument that Australia and South Africa should stop shark-cage-diving not only for the sake of the safety of people but also for the welfare of the great white shark is strengthened by showing that elsewhere this shark is protected from interference. In other words, Australia and South Africa should be consistent with 'most parts of the world'.

(A) might give us evidence that would support the concern over the danger of the great white. But it is evidence that is difficult to work with. We are told that California has already banned shark-cage-diving, and how this links with the evidence of the fatality in August 2004 is unclear. Anyway, we don't know whether this particular month was unusual for fatalities (whether the numbers are relatively high or low). In this way, we don't know whether or not the evidence provides further support for the argument.

(C) is insufficient evidence to provide further support for the argument. It clarifies the meaning of the claim 'The number of attacks ... has been increasing' but does not add any further evidence to make the argument stronger.

(D) could be used to make the argument stronger. This would be by being used to argue that there are opportunities to be close to sharks without using the shark cage method. But the evidence is insufficiently developed for us to be sure whether or not it would be consistent with the argument. For example, it could be that the author would see this practice of swimming with small reef sharks as being similarly problematic in putting humans and sharks together unnaturally.

ACTIVITY 5: COMMENTARY

The author argues that people's efficiency at work is reduced if they feel the need to respond to e-mails and texts as soon as they get them. This reason is used to conclude that employers 'should take steps to stop their staff' responding in this way.

(A) is evidence which supports the claims that the problem of 'infomania' is widespread. However, it does not strengthen the particular reason that the author uses to support the conclusion.

(B) does provide further evidence to support the reason. We have to assume that an increased rate of stress and number of arguments at work is a bad thing for employers, but it doesn't seem unreasonable to make this assumption. Seen in this way, this evidence would provide further evidence for reduced efficiency at work.

(C) is evidence that goes counter to the author's conclusion. It provides further evidence of the problem of 'infomania' by showing that employers encourage it.

(D) also provides evidence of the extent of 'infomania'. Though we could see this evidence as strengthening the concern about the widespread nature of the problem, it does not strengthen the reason that the author uses for employers to take steps to stop staff responding to e-mails and texts as soon as they get them.

REFERENCES

(1) See 'Cheats blame rotten teaching', *The Times Education Supplement*, 15 April 2005

(2) Quoted in Michael Billig, *Arguing and thinking: a rhetorical approach to social psychology* Cambridge University Press, 1989, p 95

(3) 'Liberty and consistency are going up in smoke,' *The Times*, 23 October 2002

9
PULLING IT ALL TOGETHER

This chapter is going to be mostly concerned with giving you opportunities to practise what we've been doing. The Unit 4 paper requires you to answer questions on an authentic piece of argumentation. This is likely to come from a source like one of the more serious UK newspapers such as *The Times*. Unlike much of the material that you worked on at AS level, this will not have been put together for assessment purposes. It will have been written without a necessary regard for tidy structure and balance.

You will have to answer a set of questions based on such an article. These questions could cover a wide range of skills but will always have elements of analysis, evaluation, and production of arguments. The latter arguments could well include those with an ethical component. Therefore the work we did on ethical theories for Unit 3 (Chapter 5) will also be relevant for such questions.

We'll start with an article that takes us back to the issue of what to do about the problem of violent computer games.

ACTIVITY 1

Read the following article.

Breeding evil?[1]

There's no solid evidence that video games are bad for people, and they may be positively good.

'It is an evil influence on the youth of our country.' A politician condemning video gaming? Actually, a clergyman denouncing rock and roll 50 years ago. But the sentiment could just as easily have been voiced by Hillary Clinton in the past few weeks, as she blamed video games for 'a silent epidemic of media desensitisation' and 'stealing the innocence of our children'.

The gaming furore centres on Grand Theft Auto: San Andreas, *a popular and notoriously violent cops and robbers game that turned out to contain hidden sex scenes that could be unlocked using a patch downloaded from the internet. The resulting outcry (mostly from Democratic politicians playing to the centre) caused the game's rating in America to be changed from 'mature', which means you have to be 17 to buy it, to 'adults only', which means you have to be 18, but also means that big retailers such as* Wal-Mart *will not stock it. As a result the game has been banned in Australia; and, this autumn, America's Federal Trade Commission will investigate the complaints. That will give gaming's opponents an opportunity to vent their wrath on the industry.*

Scepticism of new media is a tradition with deep roots, going back at least as far as Socrates' objections to written texts, outlined in Plato's Phaedrus. *Socrates worried that relying on written texts, rather than the oral tradition, would 'create forgetfulness in the learners' souls, because they will not use their memories; they will trust to the external written characters and not remember of themselves.' (He also objected that a written version of a speech was no substitute for the ability to interrogate the speaker, since, when questioned, the text 'always gives one unvarying answer'. His objection, in short, was that books were not interactive. Perhaps Socrates would have thought more highly of video games.)*

Novels were once considered too low-brow for university literature courses, but eventually the disapproving professors retired. Waltz music and dancing were condemned in the 19th century; all that twirling was thought to be 'intoxicating' and 'depraved', and the music was outlawed in some places. Today it is hard to imagine what the fuss was about. And rock and roll was thought to encourage violence, promiscuity and satanism; but today even grannies buy Coldplay albums.

Joystick junkies

The opposition to gaming springs largely from the neophobia that has pitted the old against the entertainments of the young for centuries. Most gamers are under 40, and most critics are non-games-playing over-40s. But what of the specific complaints—that games foster addiction and encourage violence?

There's no good evidence for either. On addiction, if the worry is about a generally excessive use of screen-based entertainment, critics should surely concern themselves about television rather than games: American teenage boys play video games for around 13 hours a week (girls for only five hours), yet watch television for around 25 hours a week. As to the minority who seriously overdo it, research suggests that they display addictive behaviour in other ways too. The problem, in other words, is with them, not with the games.

Most of the research on whether video games encourage violence is unsatisfactory, focusing primarily on short-term effects. In the best study so far, frequent playing of a violent game sustained over a month had no effect on participants' level of aggression. And, during the period in which gaming has become widespread in America, violent crime has fallen by half. If games really did make people violent, this tendency might be expected to show up in the figures, given that half of Americans play computer and video games. Perhaps, as some observers have suggested, gaming actually makes people less violent, by acting as a safety valve.

Neophobes unite

So are games good, rather than bad, for people? Good ones probably are. Games are widely used as educational tools, not just for pilots, soldiers and surgeons, but also in schools and businesses (see article). Every game has its own interface and controls, so that anyone who has learned to play a handful of games can generally figure out how to operate almost any high-tech device. Games require players to construct hypotheses, solve problems, develop strategies, learn the rules of the in-game world through trial and error. Gamers must also be able to juggle several different tasks, evaluate risks and make quick decisions. One game, set in 1930s Europe, requires the player to prevent the outbreak of the second world war; other games teach everything from algebra to derivatives trading. Playing games is, thus, an ideal form of preparation for the workplace of the 21st century, as some forward-thinking firms are already starting to realise.

Pointing all this out makes little difference, though, because the controversy over gaming, as with rock and roll, is more than anything else the consequence of a generational divide. Can the disagreements between old and young over new forms of media ever be resolved? Sometimes attitudes can change relatively quickly, as happened with the internet. Once condemned as a cesspool of depravity, it is now recognised as a valuable new medium, albeit one where (as with films, TV and, yes, video games) children's access should be limited and supervised. The benefits of a broadband connection are now acknowledged, and politicians worry about extending access to the have-nots. Attitudes changed because critics of the internet had to start using it for work, and then realised that, like any medium, it could be used for good purposes as well as bad. They have no such incentive to take up gaming, however.

Eventually, objections to new media resolve themselves, as the young grow up and the old die out. As today's gamers grow older—the average age of gamers is already 30—video games will ultimately become just another medium, alongside books, music and films. And soon the greying gamers will start tut-tutting about some new evil threatening to destroy the younger generation's moral fibre.

© The Economist Newspaper Ltd, London 2005

Evaluate the argument and, where you can, give its structure.

The next article has all sorts of things going on in it. It's another authentic one, this time on the subject of drug control.

ACTIVITY 2

Hit the drug users. It's that simple.[2]

If the war on narcotics is failing, then giving up isn't the answer, says Ross Clark.

It didn't need Lord Birt and his 'blue skies' thinking to tell the Government that the war on drugs has failed miserably. In fact, anyone who tried to make out that it was being won would be seeing the sky rose-tinted, through their spectacles. As a report by the strategy unit at the Cabinet Office makes clear, the result of the global war against drugs so far has been a massive increase in drug consumption. I can quite believe Lord Birt's estimate that the cost of crime associated with heroin and crack use in Britain is £16 billion a year.

It is becoming received wisdom that the only solution is legalisation. Lift prohibition, goes the argument, and the price of drugs will fall, putting the drug barons out of business. Occasionally a further argument is added: that making things illegal merely tempts people to do them and that if prohibition were to be lifted, drugs would lose their allure.

Around dinner-party tables in London, clouded in pungent reefer-smoke, it is no doubt an easy line of thought to sustain. It is less easy when not stoned. Were illegal drugs to be legalised, their supply and distribution would presumably fall into the hands of multinational companies, just like those who sell tobacco. True, tobacco executives don't gun each other down on the streets, but they are frequently accused, often by the same people who advocate liberalisation of drugs, of peddling death to impressionable young people, especially in the Third World.

It is hard to imagine that many supporters of drug liberalisation would be pleased by the sight of Western executives touring China and Africa promoting crack cocaine.

As for the argument that prohibition gives allure to drugs, it is nonsense. Look at the relative numbers of people who drink and smoke, and those who take illegal drugs: there is no comparison. Legalisation of any illegal drug, be it cannabis, cocaine or heroin, would inevitably be accompanied by a huge rise in consumption as experimentation became much easier.

Much as I favour free-market solutions to many economic problems, this is one free market that we can well do without. Is there anyone who really fancies an increase in the squalor, violence and mental illness associated with drug taking, and to see more young lives ruined? To say that drug takers would no longer have to steal if hard drugs were legalised is foolish: it would still cost money to buy your fix of heroin, even if not quite as much. Given that heroin addicts tend to find it hard to earn money at all, you can be sure they would still end up stealing to maintain their habit.

As for the assertion that drug-dealing gangs would cease to fight each other were there no illegal drugs over which to fight, it is extremely naive. There will be plenty of other criminal openings for any drug dealers forced into a career change. The result of drug liberalisation could prove extremely hazardous to the public if, say, the drug dealers moved en masse into, say, carjacking.

The war against drugs is failing, but giving up on it is hardly the only option. There is, of course, the option of intensifying it. In spite of the fearsome resources deployed against coca growers in Colombia (which Lord Birt says has merely switched the industry to Bolivia), in some respects the war against drugs has been extremely feeble. When he was justifying war against the Taleban in 2001, Tony Blair made the astonishing claim that Britain was sending in the troops partly in order to suppress the heroin industry. In fact, it was the Taleban who had suppressed heroin growing, and us, after the war, who failed to tackle its resurgence.

But there is little point in engaging in a war against drugs if we are going to tackle only supply and do so little to fight demand. What effort is going into the punishment of users of illegal drugs? None at all. On the contrary, drug users are increasingly seen as victims, who have no power to resist what is pushed at them by evil dealers and should in no circumstances be saddled with a criminal record.

Ann Widdecombe, the former Shadow Home Secretary, was scorned for daring to suggest that anyone caught in possession of cannabis should be fined £100. I have never understood what was wrong with her suggestion. We prosecute those who buy stolen goods, not just those who steal them. We prosecute those who view child porn on the internet, not just the porn merchants. Why are we so feeble at prosecuting those who encourage drug dealers by buying their product? Admittedly, it would be counterproductive to send drug users to prison when our jails are awash with drugs. But dope smokers forced to do community service with the mentally ill (many who gained their affliction by smoking dope), crack dealers forced to help victims of street crime? Why not?

The negative outcome of Prohibition of liquor in America in the 1920s should not blind us to the fact that a war against hard drugs has been fought once – and won.

Parts of Britain in mid-Victorian times, most notably the Fens, were plagued by opium addicts. One chemist in Wisbech was found to have 40 gallons of laudanum in stock. Wisbech, not coincidentally, had a infant mortality rate worse than inner-city Liverpool. Yet between the 1870s and 1920s opium taking in Britain was almost entirely eradicated, through a combination of restriction of supply and suppression of demand.

If it can be done once, it can be done again. But it will take more than just a campaign against Yardies and South American farmers to succeed. Above all, we should stop treating drug takers as helpless victims, and instead make them responsible for their actions. The drugs problem lies as much with middle class recreational users as it does with Third World farmers who grow illegal drugs and British gangs who trade in them.

Evaluate this argument.

You're now ready for the big one. You have all the skills (and knowledge) you need to tackle an authentic passage with questions attached to it like you'll meet in an exam. Have a go at doing the next exercise. You'll find the answers given at the end of this chapter. (At the end of each question, you'll find an indication of the number of marks that will be given for that question.)

ACTIVITY 3

A big, plump target for Gordon[3]

My Big Issue by Christina Odone

It would take a brave politician to levy a fat tax, but we'd all be in better shape for it.

...

Welcome to fat Britain, where one in three adults is overweight or obese, and where childhood obesity has increased threefold in 20 years. England has the fastest increasing weight problem in Europe, and comes third only to America and Australia in the developed world in terms of the percentage of the population that ranks as overweight. The nation's expanding waistline is not only unsightly but it is unhealthy, and uneconomical.

Fat-related illnesses and diseases cost the NHS £7.4 billion a year. Here, then, is something for our politicians to sink their teeth into. Poll after poll shows that the NHS remains a crucial concern for the public. Fat should become an election issue and the party that pledges to introduce a fat tax will win huge approval ratings — it will be seen as daring to take on, Jamie Oliver-style, the giants of the food industry and the pushers of fast food.

Over the past few years politicians have tiptoed around the fat tax: it was, everyone agreed, unpopular and unworkable. But we heard this defeatist talk about school dinners, too. We were told that any change in menus would run into formidable opposition: parents wouldn't stand for it, the dinner ladies wouldn't cope, the pupils would rebel. Yet, one television series later, school dinners look set to be revolutionised. Impose a fat tax and the same can be true of Britons' eating habits outside the school walls.

163

Far from being a crackpot notion that could be implemented only in a Scandinavian nation the size of a pocket handkerchief, the fat tax is already in place in some parts of the United States, where the US Surgeon-General declared obesity an epidemic back in 2001. Nineteen states, including New York and California, already levy special taxes on snack foods, sweets and soft drinks. It's a recent scheme, so the jury is still out as to its impact on the nation's health (and weight); but, according to The Economist's 2003 food survey, the scheme has proved eminently workable, and is already generating healthy revenues.

In Britain, the Wanless report last year ranked obesity, along with smoking and alcohol, as a major cause of preventable chronic illness, but stopped short of recommending any kind of regulation of the food industry. Wanless, like new Labour, was wary of giving rise to a libertarian chorus decrying the nanny State. Indeed, when the tax was last mooted, in 2003, by the Prime Minister's Strategy Unit, the Food and Drink Federation immediately condemned it as unacceptable and unworkable interventionism. Yet to change the lifestyle of a nation (or a third of the nation, in this case) we cannot rely simply on government advertising or more television programmes starring cheeky chefs.

The Government's decision to wage war on drink-driving and smoking immediately resulted in a punitive tax on these goods. A nation that can accept to pay a few pennies more for its drink and its fags will not balk at paying extra for its Twix. This is all the more so when we learn of the benefits of a reduction in fat consumption: according to the Wanless report, the nation can save £30 billion by 2022–23 if we reduce the incidence of fat-related diseases. Meanwhile, Oliver's shock tactics showed how a ban on junk food affected children's attention span, mood swings and hyperactivity.

The campaign for a fat tax has long been caricatured as promoting body fascism or Soviet-style interventionism. It is neither; it is a campaign against injustice. Obesity overwhelmingly affects the poorest members of society. They are the ones who are most likely to be health illiterate; as Oliver's School Dinners showed, there are children out there who have never seen an aubergine. They are the target market of the cheap'n'fat food producers, who know that as long as Turkey Twizzlers cost £2.98 per kilo, only the health-conscious will buy turkey thighs at £4.98 a kilo.

A fat tax, whose revenue would be reinvested in the NHS (benefiting its predominantly low-income users), would tilt the balance in favour of fresh and unprocessed food and against tempting but nutritiously trashy morsels.

The fat tax will tackle another grave injustice. Overweight Britons, who suffer a far higher incidence of heart disease, diabetes and even cancer, occupy the beds, have the blood tests, and undergo the operations that are often denied the rest of us by a cash-strapped NHS. Why should the nation's tubbies, who choose to snack on too many crisps and walk only a few metres a day, cheat those citizens who are the unwitting victims of their medical condition rather than its architects? So forget ASBOs, the Child Trust Fund and the NHS lifestyle gurus we were promised in the last public health White Paper. A canny politician will ditch the gimmicks and go for the hard stuff. The fat tax can take up where Oliver left off, and fight the flab fast and easily. Britain will be trimmer and healthier as a result. And the NHS may get a new lease of life.

© Cristina Odone, 2005

(1) The author welcomes us to 'fat Britain'. In doing so, she gives a description of what this country looks like.

   (a) How does the evidence she provides on 'fat Britain' enable us to see what criteria she uses to determine whether or not a country is 'fat'? **[4]**

   (b) In using evidence on 'fat Britain', what must the author assume about the significance of this evidence in relation to

   (i) that from other countries **[2]**

   (ii) the significance of any increases in percentages and proportions? **[3]**

(2) (a) In paragraph 4 the author refers to what she calls 'the fat tax' being popular, and yet in paragraph 5 she describes it as 'unpopular'. Explain, with reference to the content of the argument, the extent to which the two positions are contradictory. **[7]**

   (b) In paragraph 5, the author sees the consequences of the fat tax as analogous to those of the campaign by Jamie Oliver to improve school dinners.

   (i) Identify these consequences. **[2]**

   (ii) Evaluate the analogy in three ways. **[6]**

(3) In paragraph 6, Tηε Εψονομιστ's 2003 food survey is referred to as saying that the fat tax scheme in the US is 'eminently workable' and is 'already generating healthy revenues'.

   (a) What meaning of 'workable' would be relevant in this context? **[2]**

   (b) Explain why the generation of 'healthy revenues' might be inconsistent with a fat tax being 'eminently workable'. **[3]**

(c) In paragraph 7, the author supports the idea of changing 'the lifestyle of a nation'. Explain how her enthusiasm for 'healthy revenues' could be both consistent and inconsistent with changing the nation's lifestyle. **[4]**

(4) In paragraph 7, the author is critical of the Wanless report for not 'recommending any kind of regulation of the food industry.'
Produce an argument that
(a) shows that such regulation and a fat tax are alternative strategies, **[5]** and
(b) shows how each can be more justifiable than the other. **[8]**

(5) In paragraph 8, the author links the idea of a fat tax with the Government's policies against drink-driving and smoking. Give four reasons why there are differences between, on the one hand, drink-driving and/or smoking, and on the other, products such as Twix. **[8]**

(6) In paragraphs 9 and 11, the author refers to 'injustice'.
(a) If we take a definition of injustice to be centrally concerned with 'unfairness', examine how this applies to the two occasions when the author uses it. **[5]**
(b) Show how, especially in paragraph 9, the fat tax would be unjust to the poor. **[3]**
(c) Show how the fat tax as discussed in paragraph 10 would deal with the problem of injustice as raised in paragraph 11. **[2]**

So that's it all done. We've been on quite a journey together. It's been a bit like going round an aquarium at a large zoo. And we've met some exotic fish on the way. There we saw that deontological creature, worrying what it should do (but knowing really). There was a Nozickean one, keeping itself to itself. There was the Rawls fish hiding behind some weed. In the deductive tank, we came across different syllogisms, with their curious names. A *modus ponens* swimming alongside a *modus tollens*: what a well-matched pair they make. More recently we've met charity, indifference, and humanity in the principles tank, although we couldn't see the excluded middle we were told might have been there.

Perhaps enough's enough now. We could have gone to look at the next tank with things like the fallacy of the ambiguous middle and *argumentum ad baculum* in it. But perhaps another day, we'll come back and look for them. Thanks for your company. Enjoy the rest of the day.

ACTIVITY 1: COMMENTARY

The first, third, and fourth paragraphs are concerned with establishing (by examples) that the old have traditionally been suspicious of the young. These examples are then used to support the claim in the fifth paragraph that 'The opposition to gaming springs largely from the neophobia [fear of the new] that has pitted the old against the entertainments of the young for centuries.' Evidence on the age of gamers and their critics is given to lend further support to this claim.

The second paragraph gives us information relevant to the debate on the nature of the computer games 'problem'.

So what has the author achieved at this stage?

The historical evidence that the old have traditionally been suspicious of the activities of the young has its limitations. There might well be particular historical contexts that need to be considered and, of course, even if such evidence can be provided this does not mean that there might not still be a good case against violent computer games.

In the sixth paragraph the author addresses the first part of the question 'what of the specific complaints – that games foster addiction and encourage violence?' They dismiss the charge of addiction in two ways. Firstly, if we take time spent at an activity as the measure, then TV is much more addictive, given the number of hours spent watching it compared to the number spent playing games. Secondly, the author argues that those who spend many hours playing games 'display addictive behaviour in other ways'. Thus it is not the games as such that are the problem.

How would we respond to this evidence? The evidence on TV-watching needs to be considered in the light of the fact that watching TV tends to be a normal family activity. It would not be surprising if games players watched more TV than played games. We would perhaps be more interested in the number of hours spent playing games rather than other activities (sport or socialising perhaps).

The evidence that those who spend a lot of hours playing games show addictive behaviour in other ways is certainly relevant. It can be used to show that just because some games players spend a lot of time playing games does not mean that therefore games are addictive. However, one could consider that games could reinforce addictive behaviour (if one considers evidence that shows that brain chemistry can be affected by this activity).

Paragraph seven looks at the second part of the question asked at the end of paragraph five. It does this in three ways. The first is to provide evidence that any change in the level of aggression had only short-term effects. This is relevant evidence, but it cannot escape the counter-claim that even short-term increased aggression could be a problem. The second is to show that violent crime has fallen during the time that gaming has become widespread in the US. There could be many responses to this use of evidence. You might want to argue that violent crime could have fallen even further if it had not been for the games being played. You could argue that there could be lots of other explanations for the decline in violent crime. For the intriguing one that it was abortion that has caused the drop in violent crime in the US (by losing those people who would have gone on to commit crime) see the book 'Freakonomics' [4]. The claim that gaming could act 'as a safety valve' is an interesting one, but no evidence is provided for it.

Paragraph eight begins with the question 'So are games good, rather than bad, for people?' The rest of the paragraph has a straightforward structure of an argument.

R1: 'Games are widely used as educational tools … businesses.'
R2: 'Every game has its own interface … high-tech device.'
R3: Games require players to construct hypotheses … trial and error.'
R4: 'Gamers must be able to juggle … quick decisions.' (evidence provided)
C: 'Playing games is thus an ideal form of preparation for the workplace of the 21st century.'

The author uses these reasons to support their claim that good games are probably good for people. Of course, the obvious response is to say that, though all the reasons in this part of the argument can be accepted as good reasons, they do not deal with a possible counter-argument about the effect of 'bad' games.

In the ninth paragraph, the author returns to the original point that opposition to games is really a generational thing. They use the example of the internet to show that when the older generation can quickly see an advantage in a technological change, then their attitude to it changes. You might want to consider whether this is a relevant point.

In the end, the author makes the (perhaps inevitable, given their argument) point that games will be accepted just because gamers themselves will get old.

ACTIVITY 2: COMMENTARY

There are lots of things to spot in this argument.

The second paragraph has a developed counter-argument in favour of legalisation of drugs.

R1: with legalisation, 'the price of drugs will fall, putting the drug barons out of business.'

R2: 'if prohibition were to be lifted, drugs would lose their allure.'

The third paragraph seeks to respond to R1. It begins with an example of an *ad hominem* argument, moves into a sort of hypothetical argument, and also offers a straw man in the last sentence. After all that, it doesn't really address R1!

The fourth paragraph seeks to respond to R2. The first point doesn't really do much. Just because more people smoke and drink (both legal) than take illegal drugs doesn't disprove R2. We would be interested to look at smoking and drinking rates for those for whom these activities are illegal, in that these would be more relevant evidence. The second point that legalisation would inevitably lead to 'a huge rise in consumption' is not developed, even though the explanation 'as experimentation became much easier' is given.

The next paragraph has something of another straw man and rhetoric about it, in that obviously nobody is going to fancy 'an increase in the squalor, violence and mental illness associated with drug taking.' The second point has more merit: whatever the price of drugs there could be a problem of crime with those who are addicted stealing to get money for their drugs.

The next paragraph has an oddity in it. There is nothing to demonstrate that drug liberalisation could have the consequence of leading to greater carjacking (even though it is given as a hypothetical).

The seventh paragraph starts with something of a false dilemma: either give up on the war against drugs or intensify it. We could do things differently. We could target some groups rather than others. We could concentrate on drug gangs.

The ninth paragraph has the analogy of how we respond to people who buy stolen goods. It also has the one about how we respond to people who view 'child porn on the internet'. You should consider whether these are useful analogies. Are the situations sufficiently similar? You could, for example, look at the issue of addiction here (thus bringing in issues of knowledge and responsibility).

The evidence in paragraph ten is used to infer that we can control drugs. The counter-example of Prohibition is rejected by stressing the example of how opium use in Britain in the nineteenth and early-twentieth centuries was controlled by both restricting supply and suppressing demand. To what extent can this evidence be used? How can we see its significance? What explanation can we provide? Is it relevant to our society?

In the end, has the author shown that the solution is to 'hit the drug users.' Is it 'that simple'?

ACTIVITY 3: COMMENTARY

(1) (a)

The criteria are

- the proportion of a country that is overweight or obese;

- the rate of increase of childhood obesity;

- the rate of increase of a 'weight problem' in relation to other countries;

- the ranking of a country in terms of the percentage of its population that is overweight.

    (1 mark for each correct point)

(b) (i)

- The definitions of 'overweight and obese' are the same/largely the same for each country that is used.

- The information from other countries on the population that is 'overweight and obese' is reliable. (This could be expressed in a number of ways, each of which would count as an assumption.) These are as follows.

- The information is collected regularly.

- The information is collected accurately.

- The information is published in a way that doesn't bring in any distortion.

   (1 mark for each correct point)

(ii)

- The (threefold) increase in childhood obesity in Britain cannot be explained in terms of a (very) low starting point.

- The (threefold) increase in childhood obesity in Britain is not less/more than the increase in other countries.

- The (threefold) increase in childhood obesity in Britain is not to be understood in terms of a proportionate increase in the number of children.

- The rate of increase of the weight problem in England cannot be explained in terms of a (very) low starting point.

   (1 mark for each correct point)   **[9]**

(2) (a)

The author argues for the popularity of the fat tax in two ways:

The cost to the NHS of 'fat-related illnesses and diseases' is linked to the findings from polls that the NHS is a crucial issue for the public. (1 mark for first point; 1 mark for second)

It will be seen as 'daring to take on … the giants of the food industry and the pushers of fast food.' (1 mark)

The author doesn't argue for the unpopularity of the fat tax (1 mark); she does no more than state that 'over the past few years … everyone agreed' that it was 'unpopular'. (1 mark) She then goes on to argue why, as a result of the school dinners' campaign, things would now be different. (1 mark)

As a result, the two positions are not contradictory, in that, whereas popularity is argued for, unpopularity is seen as something that was once the case, but no more. (1 mark)**[7]**

(b) (i)

The consequences of the fat tax are that 'Britons' eating habits' (outside the school walls) would be 'revolutionised'. The consequences of the Jamie Oliver campaign would be 'revolutionised' school dinners. (1 mark for each correct point)

- With improved school dinners, there are presumably limited opportunities within school to eat those that are not improved. Whereas the fat tax might have far more limited effects on eating habits because the range of choices of food outside school remains the same.

- By reducing the appeal of certain unhealthy products through the effect on their cost, the fat tax could limit the choice of what food to have such that people chose more healthy products. This would be similar to the restriction of school dinners to healthy versions.

- The author exaggerates the nature of the difficulty of introducing healthy school dinners (protest from parents and pupils; dinner ladies not coping), in that schools are a relatively easily controlled environment. However, she underestimates the difficulties of ensuring that a fat tax changing people's eating habits, in that the same range of food continues to be available.

(2 marks for each correct evaluation, made up of one mark for consideration of school dinners and one for consideration of the fat tax in relation to each evaluation) **[8]**

(3) (a)

'Workable' would have the meaning of 'being able to target the specific products (foods and drinks) which are most likely to contribute to the problem of obesity'

It could also mean that the tax is at a sufficient level to act as a deterrent on consumption.

(2 marks for one correct point) **[2]**

(b)

The word 'healthy' as applied to revenues means something like 'at a usefully high level'. The problem with such high levels of revenue is that they appear to indicate that the fat tax is not sufficiently deterring people from consuming the problem products. In this way, a fat tax that is good at raising revenue is one that doesn't make the right impact on the problem of obesity, so is not very 'workable'.

The problem could be encapsulated for the third mark as the conflict between purpose and outcome.

(1 mark for appropriate meaning of 'healthy revenues'. 1 mark for correct

identification of the problem of healthy revenues in relation to deterrence.1 mark for showing why there is a conflict between 'healthy revenues' and 'eminently workable')

[3]

(c) Consistent:
Many overweight people are sufficiently deterred from buying many (any) unhealthy products to produce a change in the nation's lifestyle. However, those who continue to buy these products in sufficiently large quantities ensure that the extra revenue raised by the fat tax could be described as 'healthy'.

Inconsistent:
If the lifestyle of the nation is changed in the way the author wants, then not enough people are buying the products that attract the fat tax. As a result, healthy revenues show that the lifestyle of the nation hasn't been sufficiently changed.

(2 marks for each adequately-developed point)   [4]

(4) (a)

Regulation of the food industry could be seen as an alternative strategy to a fat tax.

This is because the fat tax seeks only to make certain products less attractive to potential consumers through higher prices. It doesn't seek to take such products off the shelves, except inasmuch as higher prices (it is hoped) reduce consumption and therefore the incentive for shops to stock them. In this way, the fat tax is a strategy that can be pursued without any regulation of the food industry.

(3 points made above, each attracting one mark)

However, regulation of the food industry could be seen as a way of avoiding the need for a fat tax. If the food industry is required to sell only those products that do not contribute to the problem of obesity (or at least stop producing the worst of these), then the notion of a fat tax would be much more difficult to justify.

(2 points made above, each attracting one mark)   [5]

(b)

Credit to be given for the content of the argument.

- Regulation is more justifiable than a fat tax because it
- ensures people do not eat certain types of unhealthy food;
- ensures people are more likely to eat (more) healthy food.

The consequences for the nations' health are therefore more certain. In this way, the consequences of the policy are a good way of justifying it. The consequences are positive both for individuals (who enjoy better health and well-being) and for society (less ill-health to treat).

A fat tax is more justifiable than regulation because it

- allows people to make choices between foods in part based on price;

- raises revenue that can be used for useful social expenditure.

The consequences for the nation's health are less certain perhaps than with regulation, but the fat tax treats people with respect for their preferences, unlike regulation which prevents them from exercising preferences.

(4 marks for each section, with credit given for reasoning that leads to a judgement in each case; thus total marks = 4 x 2) **[8]**

(5)

- Any single episode of drink-driving can have potentially very serious consequences, unlike small consumptions of products such as Twix.

- No single episode of drink-driving can be justified, whereas there is no such problem with low consumption of products such as Twix.

- Some products such as Twix could be beneficial to health in small quantities, unlike drink-driving.

- Smoking cigarettes can lead to addiction, unlike products such as Twix.

(You could probably think of more.)

(2 marks for each correct point, each mark coming from each component) **[8]**

(6) (a)

Paragraph 9: If we take the author to be saying that it is unfair that the poorest members of society are obese, there must be a way in which they are being treated in ways that are not fair. This would be because (as she says) the poor are denied information about health and food. It would also be because they're too poor to afford more healthy food. It is thus unfair that they are excluded from healthy living in two (preventable) ways. (3 marks)

Paragraph 11: If we apply the meaning of 'unfairness' here, the author is saying that it is unfair that overweight people consume a disproportionate amount of NHS resources. The author compounds the unfairness by arguing that it is the fault of those who are overweight that they are in this condition. Being preventable through exercise and healthy eating, the condition of being overweight is one that requires us to allocate resources unfairly. (3 marks) **[5]**

(b)

Paragraph 9 details how the poor are the target market for unhealthy food. The author emphasises the problem by showing that healthy food is much more expensive. In that a fat tax would presumably tax the unhealthy food, but not bring the price down of the healthy food, the poor would simply have to pay more for their unhealthy food, whatever food they eat. (3 marks) **[3]**

(c)

The fat tax would raise money from the low-income high consumers of unhealthy food and would then be used to pay for the extra NHS resources needed by this group. In this way, the unfairness that they take resources away from those who are not overweight is dissolved: they pay for their own health care. (2 marks) **[2]**

REFERENCES

(1) *The Economist*, 6 August 2005

(2) *The Times*, 4 July 2005

(3) *The Times*, 18 April 2005

(4) S Levitt (and S Dubner), *Freakonomics*, Allen Lane, 2005, Chapter 4

NOTES

NOTES

NOTES

Critical Thinking AS Level

Roy van den Brink-Budgen

This book is designed specifically for students and teachers of AS Level Critical Thinking Units 1 and 2 and provides comprehensive coverage of OCR's new AS specification in Critical Thinking.

In one volume, it covers:

Unit 1. Credibility of evidence; how context can affect credibility; issues of perception, language, interpretation, and judgement; different types of evidence; results of bias; possible weaknesses and strengths; using a credibility calculus; judging a case.

Unit 2. Assessing and developing argument; what forms arguments can take; the nature of conclusions; assumptions and evidence; evaluating arguments; special kinds of argument content; producing arguments.

Critical Thinking for AS Level includes a complete range of topics for both units of the OCR exam and provides very clear explanations of all the terms that the student will need, reinforced by examples throughout. It also provides a large number of exercises that the student can use to practise their understanding.

Critical Thinking for AS Level also provides teachers with the support they need to teach OCR's AS Level Critical Thinking syllabus.

ISBN 1 84528 085 7

Critical Thinking for Students
Learn the skills of critical assessment and effective argument
Roy van den Brink-Budgen

Critical Thinking is a core skill needed to make all your studies more effective. This totally revised and updated book is a must if you want to find out how to develop your own arguments and evaluate other people's.

'Much attention is now given to the subject of 'thinking skills' or 'core skills'. The idea behind this emphasis on such skills is that, whatever the specific subject you are studying, you are going to be using skills common to many subjects. So, if you can develop and improve these skills, then your performance in the subjects you are studying should also be developed and improved.'

Roy van den Brink-Budgen

'When teaching for the OCR AS-level course I found this an ideal book – the right depth for teachers and the right length for students. It is written with such obvious enthusiasm for lucid and practical thinking that it can be recommended to teachers and students in any field.' – *Roger Sutcliffe, President, Sapere*

ISBN 1 85703 634 4

How To Books are available through all good bookshops, or you can order direct from us through Grantham Book Services.

Tel: +44 (0)1476 541080
Fax: +44 (0)1476 541061
Email: orders@gbs.tbs-ltd.co.uk

Or via our website
www.howtobooks.co.uk

To order via any of these methods please quote the title(s) of the book(s) and your credit card number together with its expiry date.

For further information about our books and catalogue, please contact:

How To Books
3 Newtec Place
Magdalen Road
Oxford OX4 1RE

Visit our web site at
www.howtobooks.co.uk

Or you can contact us by email at info@howtobooks.co.uk